Tales of a Dude Wrangler

By

GENE HOOPES

With an introduction by *Charles Franklin Parker*

and illustrations by *George Phippen*

INKWELL BOOKS
Writing-Publishing-Printing

This book is published by Inkwell Books, under exclusive license from Beatrice Media, Inc.

First Inkwell Books printing: May 2014

Manufactured in the United States of America.

ISBN: 978-0-9766340-2-7
Library of Congress Control Number: 2018912455

Published by Inkwell Books, LLC
10632 North Scottsdale Road, Unit 695
Scottsdale, AZ 85254
Tel. 480-315-3781
E-mail info@inkwellbooksllc.com
Website www.inkwellbooksllc.com

To a loyal friend,

ROV YOUNG

Introduction

DEAR READER:

It is a pleasure to present a friend of mine, Jim Dawson. I have known him for many years as Pete, Nick, Slim, Curley, and a good many other names. His habitat is anywhere that you find the combination of range land and cattle. I have met him in the Big Horns, on the Powder, the Little Colorado, the Pecos, the Gila and the Verde. His name is legion. He is the creator and custodian of one of the richest folklore heritages of America.

You will find him at every roundup, with every sizable cow outfit, and lately, at every "dude" ranch where the real Western atmosphere lingers in the romance around the campfire.

He is as real as longhorns, boiled coffee, sourdough and jerky. He is as colorful as the radiations of the prism in a sunset; as big of spirit as the vast valleys, plains and mountains; and his lust for storytelling the equal of all tale-spinners of ages past.

Sit at the campfire and linger over that cup of strong, mellow coffee (preferably without cream or sugar), be patient and Jim will give you an evening that brings the past to you in a soft drawl that is a natural accompaniment to the wafted smoke from the dying embers of the fires of yesteryears.

CHARLES FRANKLIN PARKER

Prescott, Arizona
July 7, 1951

Table of Contents

Tales of a
Dude Wrangler

Dancing Fools

Jim Dawson had built up quite a reputation for him self, along a certain line, but that fact was as yet unknown to the latest arrival at the Lazy R Ranch. She was from the East, and this was her first visit to the fabled land of color.

Jim had taken the dudes up Rattlesnake Gulch today. It had been a hot ride, and now, after a light lunch, they were resting in the shade of an aspen. During a lull in the conversation, the newcomer asked Jim a perfectly innocent question.

"Are there really rattlesnakes up here?" she inquired. "I haven't seen any."

"Plenty of 'em," Jim returned. "Mebbe you ain't looked in the right places."

The questioner glanced anxiously about her as though expecting to discover one of the venomous tribe sneaking up on her at that very moment. A faint smile played at the corners of Jim Dawson's generous mouth, as he deftly rolled a cigarette.

"Of course," he explained, "they ain't quite as plentiful as they used to was. I've seen the time when they was as thick as ants up here. But even rattlesnakes can't stand up agin civilization."

"Well, they should be destroyed, shouldn't they?" she persisted. "They're so dangerous and so mean."

"I ain't never found 'em hard to git along with," Jim drawled. "Snakes ain't so much different from folks. Treat 'em decent, an' you ain't likely to have much trouble with 'em. Now take that time I was down in Arizona."

Jim sat comfortably on his heels, while a cloud of smoke

curled over the brim of his weathered sombrero. He was a picture of perfect contentment.

"I was punchin' cattle down there at the time," he began. "It was durin' the spring roundup, an' I'd gone up one o' them windin' canyons after some stray yearlin's. Dark ketched me before I could locate the pesky critters, an', it bein' a long ways back to camp, I figured I might as well stay where I was an' drive down in the cool o' the mornin'." The dudes edged closer, as Jim paused to roll another cigarette.

"Well," he continued, "I hobbled my hoss, threw my saddle down between a couple o' rocks, an' stretched my weary bones out to rest. Now I hadn't paid no attention to where I was puttin' up for the night, but it must've been a rattlesnake's homestead. Anyways, when I opened my eyes next mornin', I found myself right in the middle of a whole family of 'em." There were several apprehensive exclamations from the feminine members of his breathless audience, but Jim only smiled.

"Now there was Papa," he told them, "snuggled up to me on one side, an' Mama on the other. Big beauties they was, shore 'nuff. My boots had got right well snagged on cat's-claw bushes the day before, an' there was them young rattlers–must've been a dozen or more–they was amusin' themselves rippin' off them leather snags."

"What on earth did you do?" one excited listener demanded.

"The only thing a feller could do," Jim sagely replied. "Now I didn't want for that outfit to think I was lackin' appreciation o' their friendliness. So I just begun whistlin' 'Yankee Doodle.' Reckon they'd never heard that tune before. Anyways, they shore pricked up their ears. Them youngsters just rared up on their hind legs an' begun to dance. Pop an' Mom looked at me sort o' curious like, then they joined in.

"Well," Jim concluded, "that family o' diamondbacks went circlin' round me with tails rattlin' like a bunch o' Injuns at a rain dance. I kept right on whistlin' as I loosed my hoss an' throwed my saddle. An' I'm tellin' you, folks, when I said adios to that place at sunup, them critters was still dancin'."

A Difference of Opinion

It was a perfect moonlight night. The guests were gathered on the wide veranda listening to the soft melodies which came from Jim Dawson's time-worn guitar. When he finally took time out to roll a cigarette, one of the guests asked him if he had always been a cowboy.

"Nope," was the drawling reply, "not quite. My dad had a small outfit down in Texas in the early days. Ma most always went 'long to do the cookin' at roundup time. I was hatched in a chuckwagon, so I reckon you might say I growed up with cattle. I made a good 'nuff start, but I ain't been doin' so well on the finish."

"How's that?" the guest asked, as Jim lit the cigarette.

"Well," he returned, with a wry smile, "I got busted up pretty bad a few years back, an' since then I ain't done nothin' but tote strangers over the landscape, answerin' funny questions. I ain't followed cattle for so long I've most nigh forgot what they smells like."

"Ohl" exclaimed one of the feminine members of the group, "then you prefer cattle to people, I take it."

"No, I wouldn't say that," Jim drawled. "You see, there's a lot to be said for both sides."

"Then I suppose your guests become quite annoying at times, with their silly questions."

"Oh, no," Jim returned, "it ain't that bad. It's natural for 'em to be curious 'bout things they ·ain't never seen before. We gits used to it."

"I didn't notice that you shed any tears when the lady from Boston said goodbye to you yesterday," came from another guest.

"Nope, I didn't shed no tears," Jim drawled, "but I was sort o' sorry to see her leavin'. She was all right, after we got acquainted."

"Did you have to get acquainted with her, or she with you?" "Well, I don't reckon it could've been called one-sided," was the slow response.

"Can't you tell us how it worked out?" Jim thoughtfully scratched his ear before replying.

"I don't know," he said, "mebbe it wouldn't do no harm. You see, we had advance notice 'bout her bein' a big splash in society back in her home town. An' when she landed she didn't like the setup here. Refused to ride with the crowd. No, sir; had to have a special guide. An' yours respectful was elected to show the lady the scenery. I tried to argue with the Boss, but he wouldn't listen. Said the lady planned on stayin' most o' the summer, an' it wouldn't hurt nobody to let her have her way.

"Well, I sort o' enjoyed the first day 'cause I don't have to do none o' the talkin.' She 'tended to that. Hosses was her pet subject o' conversation–that is, if you could call it by that name.

"Now I'm right fond o' hosses myself," Jim continued, when the laughter had subsided, "but I likes to have a chance to have my say now an' then. Well, she rambles on, tellin' me 'bout all the fine bosses she'd owned an' all the shows she'd been in, the ribbons she'd won, till I got a ringin' in my ears. 'Course, I seen the lady'd been on a hoss before, seen that right off. Fact was, she rode right well, seein' as how she'd never seen a good saddle. But we hadn't finished that first excursion 'fore I figured she knowed a hoss like a steer knows a holiday.

"Well, after a few days o' that treatment I begun to lose

interest in life. I couldn't sleep nights for that buzzin' in my ears. Well, I was down at the corral one mornin' when she comes breezin' 'long. Without so much as a "Howdy" she takes up where she left off the day before.

"Then she begins findin' fault with the hosses. I didn't say nothin' till she hits on old Barney. Now Barney ain't no prize-winner, but he's a mighty good hoss. 'Mr. Dawson,' she says, 'I can't understand why you don't have a good horse for yourself.' 'What's wrong with this hoss?' I says, gittin' a little hot under the collar.

"'Well, for one thing,' she says, 'his head's too big. I wouldn't think of owning a horse with such a head.' 'Mebbe not,' says I, 'but I reckon hosses ain't much different from human bein's.' 'What do you mean?' she says, sort o' sharp like. 'Well,' I says, 'I ain't never seen as how the size made much difference. It's what's inside a head that counts.'

"Then she says if we wanted our hosses to look like somethin', we'd cut off their manes an' tails. 'They'd look smarter,' she says. I just stares at her a minute, but she didn't look like she was jokin'. So I says to her, 'I reckon there's a lot o' folks might agree with you, mam. But, you see, out here we folks sort o' likes the way the Lord made things, an' we aim to keep 'em that way.' Well, we got 'long right well after that."

Reason Enough

Cocktails were being served on the veranda of the Lazy R one evening. Jim Dawson sat on the steps thrumming his old guitar. When the drinks were passed to him, Jim merely shook his head.

"Did you never drink, Jim?" one of the dudes carelessly asked.

"Yep," was the indifferent reply.

"Why did you quit?" the curious one persisted. Jim was silent as he prepared to roll a cigarette. He gave the impression that the subject was too painful for discussion.

"It happened a couple o' years back," he finally drawled, when the cigarette was under full blast. "Had to go to town one day for provisions. I was 'bout ready to start for home when I run into an old crony I hadn't seen in quite a spell. Reckon we spent more time in the bar than was called for—sayin' nothin' 'bout the money. An' by the time I got home that evenin' I was feelin' mighty good.

"The cook was standin' by watchin' me unload the stuff: on the kitchen table. Now that cook was a right smart-lookin' gal, tall with snappin' black eyes. She was sort o' uppish, though, an' I hadn't never botjiered with her.

"'What did you forget this time?' she says to me, when I'd unloaded.

"Don't yet know what got into me, but I turns on her an' I says. 'I ain't forgot nothin'—not even you.' An' I up an' kisses her right then an' there. I ain't drunk no liquor since."

"Why was that?" another dude inquired. "What happened?"

"Plenty," Jim ruefully answered. "As I was goin' out the

door that gal wraps the soup ladle 'round my neck. An' my Adam's apple ain't never got back to where it belongs."

Doubly Useful

"Ouch!" exclaimed one of the dudes, as she carelessly brushed against a cactus bush. "Will someone please tell me why these things have to have such horrid thorns on them?"

"Wouldn't be no cactus without 'em," Jim Dawson told her. "Them things keeps the cattle from gittin' fresh with 'em."

However, Jim could see that the questioner was not entirely satisfied with that explanation. Therefore, he felt called upon to elaborate somewhat upon the subject.

"They come in right handy for the coyotes too," he added; with all the accustomed gravity.

"Coyotes," she repeated. "Surely, coyotes don't eat those things, do they?"

"No, they don't eat 'em," Jim replied. "Don't reckon they'd make very good eatin'. But, you see, coyotes live on fresh meat. An' you know how it is, when meat gits stuck between your teeth, it's mighty uncomfortable. Well, the coyotes just use them long stickers for toothpicks."

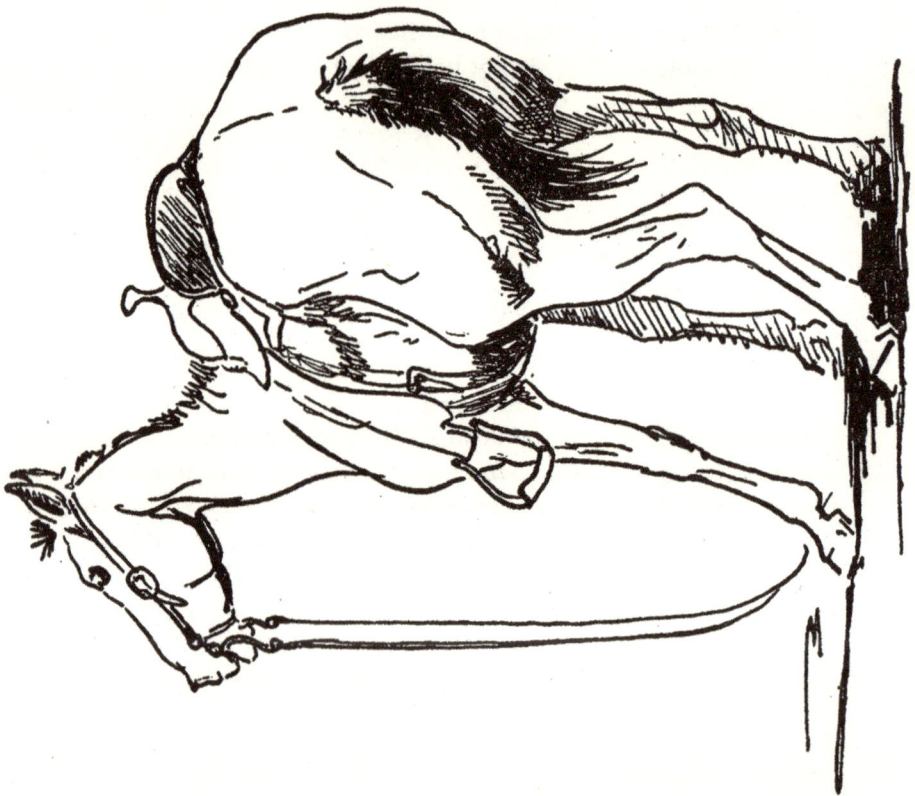

Very Deceptive

The schoolteacher had been at the Lazy R about a week. This quiet young lady from Chicago had made quite a favorable impression upon Jim Dawson. That, in all probability, was because she had not annoyed him with senseless questions.

She was at the corral this morning observing with keen interest the preparations for the day's ride. "Mr. Dawson," she finally said, watching Jim saddle a horse, "I've noticed that the horses are always mounted from the left side. Why is that?"

Jim hesitated a moment before offering an explanation. His lazy eyes brightened slowly, the temptation was irresistible. "That's because a hoss is left-handed," finally came in the usual drawl.

"Left-handed? I don't understand." She was obviously perplexed.

"Well, it's like this," Jim explained. "You see, the left legs of a hoss is a lot stronger than his right ones. An' if you was to climb up on his right side, he might fall over on you."

"Oh!" she exclaimed, "isn't that strange!"

Jim Dawson's weathered countenance was void of expression when he drawled, "Yep, just lookin' at a hoss, a person wouldn't never suspect it."

The Big City

The guests at the Lazy R had ridden up into the hills for a supper cooked over an open fire. They had showered Jim Dawson with due praise for his skill, and were now grouped about the smoldering fire waiting for the moon to rise before returning to the ranch. When Jim had strapped his meager equipment to the packhorse, he joined the group. As usual, one of the dudes had a question for him.

"Jim," he said, "I understand you don't care much for the big cities. Why is that?"

"Well," Jim drawled, easing his lean frame onto his boot heels, "I don't know where you collected your information, but I can tell you this much about it–it was one hundred per cent correct."

"But what don't you like about them?" came from one of the women of the party. Jim pushed his dusty sombrero farther back, and looked at the questioner with half-closed eyes.

"Miss," he inquired, "how long was you aimin' to stay on here?"

"Oh, I won't be leaving for a week yet," she returned, somewhat puzzled.

"Then there ain't no use me trying to tell you what I don't like about them places." The ever-ready sack of Bull Durham was brought forth, as he added, "I could tell you what I do like about 'em, that wouldn't take long."

"And what do you like about them?" she urged. "Well," Jim drawled, as he lit the cigarette, "I ain't never seen but one big city. But from what I hear there's 'bout as much difference in 'em as there is in that bunch o' steers we seen comin' up here. Anyways, there's one good thing 'bout 'em. I shore admire the way they makes it easy for a feller to git away from 'em."

"Perhaps you didn't really see the city," another dude suggested. "How long were you there?"

"Three days, miss," was Jim's reply, "an' that was exactly seventy-two hours too long. I know it was seventy-two 'cause I figured it up on the train comin' home. An' in them three days I seen plenty what wasn't no help to my appetite."

"Oh, you can't see a city in three days," she persisted. "Why, you could spend a whole day in the art gallery."

"You mean where they hang them queer-lookin' things on the walls an' call 'em pictures? I've seen them things in the Sunday papers. You look at one an' wonder if it was supposed to be a hoss or a road scraper."

"Did you ride in the subway?" someone asked.

"Nope, I shore didn't. I seen a mob o' folks pourin' into one o' them tunnels onct, like they was tryin' to outrun a prairie fire. An' I says to myself, 'Jim Dawson, you 'ain't goin' down there in that gopher hole. Supposin' that herd took a notion to stampede. Nope, you're stayin' out in the clear where you've got a chance.' I was goin' to move on when a policeman comes up to me, an says, 'Was you lookin' for somethin', stranger?' Reckon he seen by my clothes that I didn't belong there.

"Now I was sort o' took back for a minute. I'd been in the city two days, an' that policeman was the first human bein' to speak to me. But I picked up the reins, an' I says to him, 'You're right, officer; right as four aces. I'm lookin' for somethin', but I don't reckon you can tell me how to find it. You see, it's somethin' over a thousand miles from here.'

"Now you can believe it or not, folks," Jim continued, "but that policeman actually smiled. 'I can see,' he says, 'that you don't think much of our city.' 'Right agin,' I says. 'If I had to take my pick of only two places to live, here or down where it's a lot hotter, I'd have a hell of a time choosin'.'"

Jim draped his old sombrero over one ear and gazed into the distance, as though to close this painful subject of conversation. But his audience was not letting him off so easily.

"Did you see the elevated railway?" someone asked.

"Yep," was the reluctant answer, "I saw that ugly thing, makin' so much noise a feller couldn't hear himself whistle. An' I couldn't see nothin' elevatin' about it."

"How did you happen to go to the city?" another asked. Jim rolled another cigarette in silence. It looked as though he intended to ignore this question.

"Well," he finally drawled, "I was in Colorada at the time, workin' for a big hoss breeder. One day, while we was gittin' a string o' hosses ready for shippin' to Chicago, the Boss asked me how I'd like to go along with him. I was middlin' young then, an' sort o' curious, I reckon. Anyways, I says shore I'd like for to go.

"Now the gittin' there was all right. I hadn't never been on a train before an' I was sort o' high-headed, you might say, ridin' in such style. But it didn't last long. I hadn't been in that place long 'nuff to git the dust off my boots 'fore I knowed I'd made a mistake.

"I wouldn't never left our room, I don't reckon, if the Boss hadn't dragged me out. The first thing he did was to take me up on top o' some high buildin' to see the city. 'What do you think o' this?' he says to me. 'Well, Boss,' I says, 'there's only one thing on my mind right now. An' that's how we're goin' to git off this place without gittin' in that skyrocket what shot us up here.'

"Well, we got down somehow," Jim continued. "The Boss left me, so I figured I'd take a stroll to sort o' settle my stomach. I did. But I'm tellin' you, folks, I walked round the block fifteen times 'fore I got up nerve 'nuff to cross the street. I could see that if a feller didn't keep movin' he'd be tromped to death. Gosh, every time I turned round I run into somebody. It reminded me of an anthill after a hoss had tramped on it–humans millin' 'round in all directions. It didn't look to me as how they knowed where they was goin', but they shore was in a hurry to git there."

"We'd been there three days when I took sick," Jim told them, as he rolled another cigarette.

"Oh, how unfortunate!" someone exclaimed.

"Nope," Jim returned, "I ain't never figured it that way. I got up with a headache that mornin', somethin' I ain't never had before. But, you see, it was two days since I'd had a breath o' fresh air an' I hadn't seen the sun in all that time neither. I didn't eat much breakfast that mornin'. The Boss leaves me then, sayin' he won't be back till afternoon 'cause he's lookin' up an old friend.

"I was up in the room when he comes back about five o'clock. I'd been there most o' the day, not botherin' 'bout no grub. I was just sittin' there starin' out the window. There wasn't nothin' to see, 'cept a buildin' across the way, lookin' as forlorn as I was feelin'. The windows in that thing reminded me of the faces I'd seen on the street, they looked so unhappy.

"'What you been doin' today, Jim?' the Boss asks me. 'Nothin',' I says. I'm sick.' 'Sick?' 'Yep,' I tells him, 'an' I'd rather have the yellow fever than what I got now. How much longer are you aimin' to stay in this foul-smellin' corral?'

"'Heavens, man,' he says, 'why didn't you tell me before? If I'd knowed you wasn't enjoyin' yourself, we'd been out o' this damn place long ago.' And he grabs the telephone to find out when the first train leaves for Denver.

'I'm tellin' you, folks," Jim concluded, "I ain't never been so happy as when I felt that train movin an' heard the engine chuggin' off toward the settin' sun."

"Then," one of the dudes remarked, "as far as you were concerned, that trip was a dead loss."

"Nope, I wouldn't say that," Jim returned. "I reckon it taught me a couple o' things. You see, 'fore that I'd never bothered feelin' sorry for folks, 'cept when somebody lost their mother, or sweetheart. But I shore found I could spread my sympathy farther'n that. An' I've found out since that some o' them city folks wouldn't live nowheres else. So I'm right grateful to 'em, 'cause if that wasn't so, it would be gittin' some crowded out here by this time, I reckon."

A Difficult Question

A dude at the Lazy R once asked Jim Dawson what was the most difficult question he had ever been called upon to answer. Jim scratched his head thoughtfully before replying.

"Well," he finally drawled, "I reckon it was the time a lady asked me why it never rained out here."

"What did you tell her?"

"'That ain't a fair question,' I says to her, ''cause it does rain.'

"'Well, it don't look like it ever had,' she says.

"I seen she wasn't satisfied, so I says to her, 'Now all I can tell you 'bout it is what I've heard. You see, there used to be plenty o' rain in this country. That was on account o' the lnjuns havin' a feller who knowed how to bring the rains·. They called him the Rainmaker. When the first settlers come out here, them dry washes was all runnin' with water. Bu,t the white folks wasn't satisfied; they wanted the Injuns killed off. So the government sent out an army. One day there was a big battle, an' the Rainmaker was killed. Since then it only rains onct a year.'

"'An' when's that?' the lady asks me. 'Christmas, I suppose.'

"'Nope,' I says, 'it don't rain on Christmas. Only on the Rainmaker's birthday'."

An Accurate Calculation

"Mr. Dawson, is it true that a horse's age can be determined from his teeth?" That question had been put to Jim one day by an interested visitor at the corral.

"That's right, miss," Jim replied.

"But I can't understand how it would be possible," she returned.

"Well it's sort o' complicated," Jim drawled, "but I'll try an' make it clear to you, seein' as how you're interested."

The lines at the corners of Jim's mouth could have been seen to deepen, as he leisurely rolled a cigarette.

"It takes some figurin' to git at a hoss's age," he began. "First of all, you've got to find out how many minutes it takes him to eat a quart o' green oats. Then you count his teeth. When you've got them two answers you're ready to figure. Now supposin' it took him six minutes to eat them oats, an' he's got twenty-four teeth. You just divide twenty-four by six, an' you've got four. Now you multiply that by three, an' you can be mighty shore that the age o' your hoss is twelve years to a day."

Initialed

A new guest had arrived at the Lazy R that afternoon. She was sitting on the veranda steps watching the changing sunset when Jim Dawson appeared with his guitar.

"What a large mountain that is," she remarked, obviously referring to Sentinel Mountain. That majestic mass of granite was well named, standing as it did, somewhat detached from the north end of the long mesa and towering far above it.

"Yep," Jim drawled, taking his seat opposite the new guest, "Sentinel's got to be a right sizable pile o' rock in the last forty years."

There were many knowing smiles by the guests now gathering on the rose-tinted veranda. The newcomer gazed at Jim in blank amazement.

"When I first seen him," Jim said, as he extracted the Bull Durham from his shirt pocket, "he didn't look no bigger'n a good sized anthill."

The young lady gazed at Jim in silence. Fearing the subject might not be carried to its logical conclusion, one of the older guests now spoke.

"But, Jim," he said, "there must have been something wrong with your vision in those days."

"Nope," Jim returned, "my eyes was a heap sharper forty years ago than they is now."

"Well," the new guest declared, with some heat, "no one will ever convince me that a mountain can grow. I've heard that this was a land of mysteries, but I'm not accepting this as one of them."

"There ain't no mystery about it, miss," Jim assured her.

"It's just a natural as anything could be. 'Cause when I first seen old Sentinel, there was a couple o' hundred miles o' land separatin' us."

The newcomer searched Jim's impassive features a moment, then realizing that she had been duly initiated, joined in the general laughter.

Old Rambler

A party of schoolteachers from the East visited the Lazy R one summer. A few days after their arrival Jim Dawson took them up on Mule Shoe Mesa, that picturesque upheaval which lay across the vast plain like a giant rope. Far out on the plain to the west a lone mountain reared its majestic height. There were many exclamations of wonder and delight as the party gazed upon this panorama of western grandeur.

"Oh!" one enthusiastic rider exclaimed, "look at that mountain standing, there all by itself. Does it have a name, Mr. Dawson?"

"Yep," Jim replied, following her gaze with half-closed eyes, "that's old Rambler."

"Rambler," she repeated. "How did it get such an odd name?"

"It come by that name honestly, miss," Jim replied, with the faintest sparkle in his lazy eyes. "All on account of it never seemin' to be twice in the same place."

"Oh, that's impossible," declared another of the party.

"Mountains simply do not move." Jim rolled a cigarette.

"Well," he drawled, . "I ain't never seen it movin' myself, but it shore gits around. Anybody livin' in these parts will tell you the same thing."

"Why, it's incredible!" someone exclaimed.

"In which?" came from Jim, as he shifted his lazy gaze to the speaker.

"Incredible," she repeated, then added, with the teacher's instinct, "I mean it's unbelievable."

"It might seem so, miss," Jim returned, lighting a cigarette, "but them that lives 'round here ain't doubtin' it."

"But how could it move?" she demanded.

"Well," Jim drawled, "I reckon you'd better figure that out for yourself. Me, I ain't got no education, so I don't know nothin' 'bout them things they calls natural laws."

That statement was followed by silence, while the schoolteachers gazed in evident bewilderment upon Rambler Mountain. "Well, folks," Jim said, heading his horse toward the ranch, "we'd better be rustlin'."

The teachers joined the other guests on the veranda that evening, and it was soon evident that they had not forgotten the puzzling subject of the afternoon.

"Mr. Dawson," one of them said, when Jim had taken his accustomed place, "we've discussed every possible cause for the restlessness of your Rambler Mountain and we've come to the conclusion that you were only joking."

Jim flicked his cigarette and looked at the speaker in pained surprise. "Now, miss," he remonstrated, "that's somethin' Jim Dawson ain't never been knowed to do. I'll leave it to anybody that's been here more'n three days if that ain't a fact."

"I'll vouch for that," one of the male guests volunteered. "But what was the argument about?"

When the teacher, with all seriousness, had explained the situation, Jim spoke up. He was intently rolling a cigarette, taking more time than seemed necessary.

"Well," he finally drawled, "seein' as how you ain't been

able to figure it out for yourselves, I reckon I've got to do the explainin'." He flicked the match and blew a cloud of smoke into the still air. "There was a feller here a few years back what claimed to be one o' them scientists, an' he told me how it was that old Rambler could git 'round the way he does. Now I ain't sayin' the feller knowed what he was talkin' about, I'm just passin' on what he gives me.

"You see, folks, old Ramber looks like a solid pile o' rock, but he ain't. He's holler inside. All you can see is a thin shell, an' inside that shell there's some sort o' liquid. Now by midsummer the sun has got that rocky shell so all-powerful hot that the liquid inside starts boilin'. After awhile there ain't nothin' in there but gas. Old Rambler's all blowed up then, sort o' like a balloon, an' all ready to travel.

"Now you can see for yourselves how it would be. Any stout wind could slide old Rambler a mile or two over the plain, if it had a mind to."

Profound silence followed that scientific explanation. It was finally broken by one of the teachers.

"Well," she declared, with a sigh, "that is certainly the most amazing thing I ever heard."

"That's right, miss," Jim drawled, as he picked up his guitar. "Come to think on it, 'tis right amazin'."

In the Beginning

"Is it true," a dude inquired of Jim Dawson one day, "that there is a cactus which actually jumps at you, if you go near it?"

"Well," Jim drawled, "the cholla down on the desert is

sometimes called the jumpin' cactus. You can hear a lot o' yarns about the jumpin' cactus. But they're mostly from dude wranglers, the kind what was never knowed to tell the truth."

"Then they're not really dangerous?" she asked.

"No," Jim replied, "I wouldn't call 'em dangerous. Not any more."

"Please tell me about them," she urged, "how they got that way and why."

"Well," Jim began, with a faraway look in his sleepy eyes, "all I can tell you is what I've heard. I ain't had much experience with 'em myself. I got the story when I first come to this country, got it from an old Injun. Accordin' to him, the cholla didn't have no stickers in the beginnin'. They was a peaceful lot, gittin' along right well till a porcupine called on 'em one night. He 'peared like a decent sort o' feller, an' they was right glad to see him.

"Now they was gettin' along fine till porky's back got to itchin'. Then he picks out the stoutest cholla in the family an' begun scratchin' himself on it. When Mr. Porcupine waddled off home that night, the cholla found his legs was stuck full o' quills. Now it ain't hard to believe that he was hoppin' mad 'bout it. All the next day he squirms an' twists an' grunts, tryin' to git them pesky quills off.

"Well, it was a long time before he discovered that if he put all his strength onto one spot he could squeeze them quills out o' his hide. They would pop out, an' go sailin' through the air like arrows. That give Mr. Cholla an idea, an' he went to work on it. It wasn't long before he'd invented shootin' stickers that he could grow all over himself. Not bein' as selfish as some humans I've heard tell o', he give the idea to the rest o' the family. An' the chollas never had much trouble with their enemies after that."

"Oh, you surely don't believe that story!" the dude exclaimed.

"Well, miss," Jim replied dryly, "I ain't never had no call

to disbelieve it. An' I can tell you this for a fact. Them chollas ain't what they used to was. Why, I've seen the time when it wasn't safe for a feller to git within half a mile of 'em. But I reckon they're gittin' sort o' civilized too. You know, gittin' lazy an' indifferent to the dangers 'round 'em."

The Legend of Sentinel Mountain

"Is there a trail up there, Jim?" an ambitious dude once asked Jim Dawson, as he gazed up at Sentinel Mountain.

"None that I ever heard of," Jim replied.

"Hasn't anyone ever tried to climb it to the top?" the dude persisted.

"If they did, they shore never told nobody."

"Well, I think I'll try it tomorrow."

"I wouldn't if I was you," Jim advised.

"Why not?"

"'Cause you might find it unhealthy," Jim replied, rolling a cigarette with his accustomed deliberation. "Old Sentinel's got a bad reputation."

"A bad reputation for what?" the dude inquired.

"Well," Jim drawled, as he lit the cigarette, "I'll give you the story just as it was handed to me. I ain't vouchin' for it, you understand, 'cause it happened before my time. I got the story from an Injun, the same one what told me 'bout the jumpin' cactus, so I ain't never doubted it.

"Now, accordin' to the old Injun, a young brave was huntin' rabbits out here one day. All o' a sudden somethin' swooped down out o' the sky, ketched the lad by the back

"Now, accordin' to the old Injun, a young brave was huntin' rabbits out here one day. All o' a sudden somethin' swooped down out o' the sky, ketched the lad by the back o' the neck, an' flew off with him. It turned out to be a buzzard, an' he took the young Injun up on top o' old Sentinel. He dropped the brave up there an' begun callin' for his mate to come to supper.

"Well, Mrs. Buzzard never answered. More'n likely she was too busy gossipin' with some o' the neighbors to hear the old man. Anyways, Mr. Buzzard puts a rock on the young Injun's legs so he can't git away, an' then he goes sailin' off after the wife.

"Now that brave can't move his legs, but his hands is free, so he picks up a flat stone an' writes a note to his folks. He tells 'em where he is an' how he got there, and begs 'em to come git him pronto. Then he throws the rock off the mountain, hopin' somebody'll pick it up. But nobody does till old Foxear comes along a thousand years too late.

"That night the screechin' an' yellin' an' moanin' what come from the top o' old Sentinel was most nigh 'nuff to freeze the blood of an Injun. While the buzzards was feastin' themselves on Injun meat, the evil spirits come up out o' the rocks an' put a curse on the buzzards for disturbin' the peace. The next day there was nary an Injun within a hundred miles o' here. An they never come back."

"There's one bad flaw in that tale, Jim," the skeptic remarked.

"What's that?"

"No buzzard could pick up a man and fly off with him."

"Listen, son," Jim sagely replied. "Buzzards in them days was as big as airplanes. The reason they ain't so big now is 'cause o' the curse the evil spirits put on 'em. All the old ones died off before the summer was over, an' the spring crop what was just hatchin' then–well, they just never growed."

Old Rambler Settles Down

"Jim I want you to go into town this afternoon." The Boss of the Lazy R had thus addressed Jim Dawson one bright June morning. "You're to meet a guest from Boston," he continued, while Jim pulled his sombrero lower over his lazy eyes. "And watch your step, fellow, for this is no ordinary dude. She's an instructor in one of the big colleges back there. She's a noted geologist."

"A ge-which?" Jim mildly inquired.

"Geologist. One who knows all about the formation of the earth, the rocks, minerals, and all that."

"Oh," was Jim's only comment, as he ruefully rolled a cigarette. This was an assignment which was not at all pleasing to Jim. He never drove a car if it was possible to avoid it. Although it was twenty miles to town, he would always go on horseback if he had his choice. He was once heard to say, "I wouldn't trade a good hoss for the finest gas buggy ever made, with the Queen o' Sheba throwed in."

The guest from Boston was a tall, rather severe-looking person, with a mannish touch to her attire. Jim appraised her curiously, as he loaded her numerous bags into the car. It was his first encounter with this particular type, and he wondered what she would look like astride a horse. To his discomfiture, she insisted upon riding in the front seat. She appeared not to notice the village, as the car slipped through the one and only street toward the uncertain road which led to the ranch.

"Mr. Dawson," she said, as Jim shifted into high, "I can scarcely contain myself until I see that remarkable mountain I have heard so much about."

"We have a heap o' mountains here 'bouts," Jim dryly returned.

"But I refer to the one which is reputed to be transmigratory."

"Trans-which?" Jim asked, his eyes glued upon the road.

"Transmigratory," the lady from Boston repeated, glancing sternly at Jim's impassive countenance. "Movable, in simple language," she added, with a toss of her head. "I have been informed of its peculiarities, and I have made this miserable journey for the sole purpose of conducting an exhaustive study of the phenomenon."

The car hit a bad rut in the road during the brief instant Jim had taken for a sharp glance at the speaker. He barely missed a second rut, as he inquired, "Was you by any chance referrin' to Rambler Mountain?"

"Rambler," she thoughtfully repeated. "Yes, I believe that was the name. The meager information concerning tliis amazing freak of nature came to me through a friend who had seen it. If necessary, I am prepared to spend the summer in pursuit of my investigations."

"When was your friend out here?" Jim warily inquired. "I believe it was three years ago," she replied.

A close observer might have noted a slight relaxation of Jim Dawson's bronzed features and the suspicion of a smile playing about his generous mouth.

"Too bad you've had your trip for nothin'," he drawled. "Old Rambler's sort o' settled down since your friend seen him."

"What do you mean?" demanded the lady geologist from Boston.

"The old boy ain't moved out o' his tracks for more'n a year now," Jim returned.

"Please make yourself clear, Mr. Dawson."

"Well, this's how it come about," Jim began, licking his lips for want of a cigarette. "We had a big convention the spring after your friend was here."

"You mean at the ranch?"

"Nope," Jim dryly returned. "You see, this was a gopher's convention, an' there was too many of 'em to be accommodated at the ranch."

"A convention of gophers," the lady mused. "I never heard of such a thing."

"Didn't reckon as how you had," Jim remarked. "Gophers only hold conventions when the leader dies, or gits trapped. Then they gits together an' elects a new high priest. Well, this time they held their convention right 'longside o' old Rambler. Thousands an' thousands o' delegates come in from all over the country. I reckon it took a heap o' diggin' to git a hall big enough for all them delegates.

"Anyways, they worked on it for a couple o' months .. When the convention was over, they all went back home, but you can bet we didn't do no ridin' near that place. It just wasn't safe. Well, them gophers hadn't been gone long 'fore a rip-snortin' wind storm come up. It just shoved old Rambler over onto that convention ground, an' he ain't moved an inch since. A cloud o' dust blotted out the sun so bad that the chickens went to roost. Old Rambler he just settles down in that gopher hole knowin' his travelin' days was over, n• lets out one gosh-awful groan. Folks say it could be heard a hundred miles away... Right pitiful it was," Jim added, sadly, when the lady made no comment.

"Mr. Dawson," she sorrowfully exclaimed, "you can have no conception of my disappointment!"

"Yep," Jim returned, with a gleam of satisfaction in his eyes, "I reckoned as how you would be."

All the Answers

"Well, Jim, we'll have another scientist with us tomorrow." Jim Dawson, with characteristic indifference, had received that information from the Boss of the Lazy R one morning.

"That so," he replied, "What breed?"

"He's an entomologist."

"An ento-which?"

"Entomologist, one who knows all about insects. And you better not try any of your tricks on him, because he has all the answers."

Jim chuckled, as he sauntered off to the bunkhouse. "Mebbe so," he said to himself.

The professor of entomology had been at the ranch almost a week and had not yet been initiated. Some of the guests who knew Jim Dawson's weakness were beginning to wonder. Was Jim slipping, or was the professor to be let off for some unknown reason?

It was Jim's custom to take his place on the veranda steps about the time the sun dipped below the mesa. But tonight it was almost dark before he appeared with his trusty guitar.

"You're late tonight, Jim," one of the dudes reminded him. "Yep," Jim returned, with a strange note of sadness in his voice. "Mighty nigh didn't come at all."

"What was wrong?" someone asked.

"Lost an old friend," was the gloomy reply.

"Oh," another dude exclaimed. "Not your horse, I hope."

"Nope," Jim returned, slowly rolling a cigarette. "But I

thought most nigh as much o' him as I do o' old Barney. We been buddies a long time, an' I'm shore goin' to miss him."

"Was it anyone we know?" the dude inquired. "Don't reckon so," Jim replied. "Old Sol didn't git 'round much, so it ain't likely you ever seen him. But he was shore good company, 'specially durin' the winter when there wasn't much goin' on 'round here. Old Sol shore kept me from gittin' lonesome. In the evenin's he'd come out o' the wall an' sit beside me. I'd git down the old geetar, an' he'd sing as long as I kept playin'. He shore was fond o' music." Silence followed, while a cloud of smoke from Jim's cigarette drifted off in the night breeze.

"I don't believe I follow you, Mr. Dawson," a feminine member of the party remarked.

"Excuse me, miss," Jim returned, "mebbe I ain't made myself too clear. I'm a mite upset, you might say. But, you see, old Sol was a cricket an' he lived behind the stove in the bunkhouse."

Loud laughter came from the dudes who had just arrived that morning. "Oh," one of them exclaimed, "a cricket. How funny."

"Nope, nothin' funny 'bout it," was Jim's rueful reminder. The professor now spoke for the first time. "I have heard," he said, "that the cricket is noted for his adaptability."

"Adapta-which?" Jim inquired.

"Adaptability. It fits itself well into the domestic environment."

"Now mebbe I ain't followin' you too well," Jim returned. "But I can tell you this. Old Sol was no common cricket. Wouldn't be surprised, professor, if you ain't never seen the likes o' old Sol. He was smart, Sol was, an' all-powered good lookin' too. He was bright green with silver stripes down his back, an' he had red whiskers. I tell you, folks, you ain't got no idea how I'm goin' to miss the old boy. You see, we've been together more'n forty years now."

"Preposterous," the professor exclaimed.

"Pre-which?" Jim inquired, flicking his cigarette.

"Ridiculous, in other words," the professor replied.

"Crickets, like most insects, have an exceedingly brief life span. They have never been known to live more than two or three years."

"Ain't you forgittin' somethin', professor?" Jim ·drawled. "I told you· that old Sol wasn't no common cricket. He was one o' them famous Methuselum crickets."

"I never heard of any such species," the professor declared. "Mebbe not," Jim returned, "but a feller ain't never too old to learn, leastwise he shouldn't be. My old friend Foxear told me 'bout these Methuselums. He said the Injuns brought 'em along when they first come to this country. He said they always brought good luck. Now I never knowed how he got in there, but I found old Sol in one o' my saddlebags when I come out o' New Mexico way back in the nineties. He was so durned friendly that I just took him along wherever I went. I named him Solomon, 'cause he looked so wise. They tell me some o' them Methuselums can still be found in the old cliff dwellin's. Them fellers must be a thousand years old by now."

"Most extraordinary," the professor exclaimed. "Amazing, in fact. I shall have to look into this at once. I would be obliged to you, Mr. Dawson, if you would permit me to have the remains of this strange insect."

"Sorry, professor," Jim replied, "but there ain't no remains."

"I don't understand," the professor returned.

"Well, it's like this," Jim drawled, in explanation. The merest suspicion of a smile now played about his mouth. "You see, them fellers ain't aimin' to have folks git hold o' their secret. So when they finally decides to give up the ghost, they just don't leave no evidence behind 'em."

"Still don't understand," said the professor.

"Well," Jim concluded, "old Foxear told me how it was with that tribe o' crickets. They don't die like any other livin' things. They just sort o' dries up till there ain't nothin' left of 'em. Knowin' that, I was sort o' prepared, you might say. I seen as how old Sol was failin' lately, but there wasn't nothin' I could do 'bout it. Well, I was sittin' on the bunkhouse steps after supper when Sol come out. He looks up at me an' chirps a couple o' times, much as to say, 'Good-bye, Jim.' Then his eyes shut, an' he drops his head. It was right pitiful, so it was. My eyesight didn't seem too good right then. Anyways, when I could see clear I looks down at old Sol. An' believe it or not, folks, but there wasn't nothin' there but a little pile o' dust where old Sol had been sittin'."

A Superstition

The dudes were grouped about the campfire, waiting for the moon to rise. A new arrival at the Lazy R was puzzled over something she had heard.

"Is it true," she asked, "that a snake will not crawl over a hair rope?"

"That's right, miss," Jim Dawson answered, poking the fire to send a shower of sparks into the still air.

"Queer, isn't it?" the young lady mused.

"Nope," Jim returned, "there ain't nothin' queer 'bout it when you know the wherefor."

"Then what is the reason?" she eagerly inquired.

"It's all on account o' snakes bein' superstitious," Jim replied.

"Superstitious!" She laughed, mockingly.

"Yep, that's the word, miss," Jim drawled. "Snakes is 'bout

the most superstitious animals there is, 'ceptin' Injuns mebbe. Now, you see, in the beginnin' snakes was covered with hair, like all the other land farin' animals. But bein' condemned to crawl on their bellies for the rest o' time, it wasn't long 'fore they had all the hair wore off. Now, when they see a hair rope layin' on the ground, they ain't takin' no chances. They just don't go that way."

"But why not?" the dude persisted.

"'Cause,' Jim replied, "bein' superstitious, like they is, they figures as how that rope might be one o' their hairy ancestors come to life."

His Favorite

Jim Dawson had taken the dudes up on the mesa this afternoon. They were now resting in the shade of a wind-twisted juniper after the hot ride. The conversation was lagging, and, with a view to enliven it, one of the dudes who knew Jim from past experience put a question to him. Jim never entered into the general conversation of his own accord.

"Jim," the dude said, "you've been with the Lazy R a long time, haven't you?"

"Yep," Jim replied, "nigh on to twenty years now."

"You must have met some very interesting people in that time," the dude returned. "Would you mind telling us who you consider the most interesting of all those people?"

"Now I'm askin' you," Jim drawled, "is that a fair question?"

"Why not?" the dude countered. "Surely no one here expects to be in the competition."

"Well," Jim began, having been assured by his audience that such was the case. "I reckon 'bout the most interestin' person I've run into here was a young lady."

"Oh, I'm sure we all expected that," exclaimed one of the women. "She was young and beautiful, and you made love to her."

"Pardon me, miss," Jim returned, "but that's somethin' Jim Dawson ain't never done with no woman." A respectful silence followed that emphatic statement.

"I don't reckon she was what you'd call beautiful," Jim finally said. "She was middlin' young an' right good lookin', seemed to me. She landed here the first day the ranch was open, that was ten or twelve years back, an' she stayed most nigh all summer. It was a week before anybody else come along, an' we rode together every day."

"Oh, how lovely," another dude exclaimed, "riding over the hills alone for a whole week. No wonder it was interesting."

"She loved hosses an' she shore could ride 'em," Jim continued, as though there had been no interruption. "Old Barney shore took a likin' to her, but mebbe that was 'cause she always had a lump o' sugar for him."

"She must have had some sugar for you too, didn't she?" Again, Jim ignored the interruption.

"I reckon I liked her so much 'cause she was different. Yep, she was shore different. An' bein' different, the way she was, she was just 'bout the best company I ever run onto."

"Now that's all very interesting," one of the dudes remarked, as Jim paused to roll a cigarette. "But you haven't yet made it clear, to me at least, just why you found this person such excellent company."

"'Cause," Jim answered, lighting the cigarette with his usual deliberation, "'cause she was deaf and dumb."

Beyond Recognition

Jim Dawson had finished a series of songs. Laying his guitar aside, he had begun to roll a cigarette when one of the dudes on the veranda spoke.

"Jim," he said, 'I'm surprised at you."

"How's that?" Jim asked, his entire attention upon the business in hand.

"I knew you had never married," the dude returned, "and this afternoon you told us you had never made love to a woman. I never thought of you as being a woman hater."

"Who said I was a woman hater?" Jim inquired, inspecting the cigarette with an approving eye.

"Well, your remarks would certainly lead one to that conclusion."

"Sorry, folks, if them remarks o' mine was misleadin'," Jim said, as he lit the cigarette. "Facts is, I couldn't be a woman hater any more'n I could be a missionary. Now I ain't got no quarrel with women. They're all right, generally speakin'. Better'n men for the long pull, I reckon. But I just figured as how it wouldn't do me no good to be takin' a chance with 'em." "What was your objection to them?" someone asked. "Surely you're not afraid of women."

"Nope," he replied, "I ain't afraid of 'em exactly. Just ain't never been sure of 'em, I reckon."

"Were you never seriously interested in a woman?" another dude asked.

"Yep, onct," Jim admitted. "That was years back though. I'd been trottin' with her for some time an' thinkin' right well o' her till I took her to a dance one night."

"What happened at the dance?" someone asked, when Jim paused.

"Well," he drawled, "she said somethin' that wasn't exactly complimentary concernin' the green shirt I was wearin'. Then she follered that up by tellin' me she didn't like the way I combed my hair."

"And you let that discourage you!" someone exclaimed.

"I reckon you might call it that," Jim replied. "Anyways, when I got home that night, I says to myself, 'Jim Dawson, it's time you was back-trailin' 'fore it's too late. You ain't too much now, but you're likely to be a heap less 'fore that gal gits through with you.' An' I ain't never been on that kind o' trail since." "Why, the girl was only trying to help you," one of the fair ones declared.

"Mebbe so," Jim admitted, "but I hadn't been askin' for no help. An' somehow I didn't feel like bein' remodeled. Now you can see for yourselves how it might've been." He flicked the cigarette and looked appealingly at his audience. "Just supposin' I was to go out to the corral some mornin' after the wife had been workin' me over. Why, it makes me sort o' weak when I think on it. I'm tellin' you, folks, it would be downright pitiful if old Barney couldn't recognize me."

Loyalty

"I understand that cowboys are very poorly paid," a dude once remarked to Jim Dawson.

"Don't know where you got your information," Jim returned, "but I can tell you this: it ain't exactly correct. Now there was a time, an' not so long back neither, when a cowpoke didn't git more'n thirty dollars a month, generally speakin'. But if he had the sense of a gopher, he could save money at that. He only needed a couple o' dollars a month for tobacco an' onct in a long time a new pair o' boots or a shirt mebbe. Now most of 'em git a hundred dollars a month or more. Seein' as how it ain't costin' 'em nothin' for grub an' a roof over their heads, seems to me like that's durned good pay."

"I still can't see how they get along on so little," the dude persisted.

"That's only 'cause you ain't used to livin' the way we do," Jim drawled. "Now I never got more'n thirty dollars a month till just lately, an' I saved up 'nuff to buy me forty acres o' good land a couple o' hundred miles south o' here. An' it won't be long now till I've got 'nuff to retire on."

"You're leaving the ranch?" one of the dudes inquired, in surprise.

"Yep," Jim returned. "Soon's old Barney shows signs o' gittin' tired o' the job, we're headin' south. My land lays in one o' them canyons what's green most o' the year, with a good spring on it. I figure it'll be a pretty good place for Barney an' me to hole up. I'm aimin' to put up a two-room cabin for Barney an' me."

"What!" someone exclaimed, in horror. "You don't mean you intend living in the same house with a horse!"

"That's about it, miss," Jim gravely replied. "Don't know as how I've got no call to be elevatin' my nose just 'cause old Barney happens to be a hoss."

"Oh, but the odor!" someone exclaimed.

"Odor," Jim repeated, then smiled. "I reckon you mean the smell. Well, my old nose has been hit by a lot o' smells in its time. I've heard some of 'em cost a heap o' money too. They say there ain't no accountin' for tastes. Anyways, I'll take the smell of a hoss for mine, any day in the year. It's a good healthy smell." Jim exhaled a huge cloud of smoke before he went on. "We been mighty close for a long time, Barney an' me, an' I don't reckon it's goin' to hurt us to be a little closer in our old age. Barney's been packin' me 'round on his back for nigh onto fifteen years now. Looks to me like that was right close associatin', so why shouldn't we live 'longside each other?" That was an unanswerable question for the dudes. There was a profound silence.

"Barney's room," Jim continued, as he prepared to roll another cigarette, "will be all open on one side, so's he can come an' go when he sees fit. There ain't goin' to be no restrictions on the old boy. Nope, I want he should enjoy his retirement, same's I aim to do. But I'm fixin' to have him close by, so if he was to git sick in the night I'd know 'bout it. I'm tellin' you, folks, old Barney's the best friend I got. He's been a faithful friend too, an' I ain't aimin' to desert him when he gits too old to work for me."

Big Game

"Jim, what do you do," a dude inquired one evening, "when a guest becomes obnoxious?"

"Ob-which?" Jim returned.

"Obnoxious. Disagreeable, in other words."

"Well," Jim tactfully replied, "we don't often git that kind 'round here."

"But how do you handle them when they do come?"

"Leave 'em alone, an' they generally gits tired o' their own company."

"But suppose they don't?" someone asked.

"Then we try to beat 'em at their own game." It appeared

that Jim Dawson was not desirous of pursuing the subject, but the dudes were not to be denied.

"How do you mean?" one of them asked.

"Just give 'em an overdose o' their own medicine," was the drawling answer. "Like the time the big-game hunter was here." "Well," Jim said, in response to the insistence for this tale, "this feller was one o' them playboys. I guess that's what you call 'em, fellers with more money than headroom. Now he claimed he'd spent years huntin' big game in the Africa jungles. Mebbe he had, and mebbe he hadn't, but he shore did a heap o' talkin' 'bout it. Couldn't nobody git in a word crossways when he was 'round. Kept tellin' 'bout the lions an' tigers he'd killed till the crowd begun to git restless like. Some of 'em was even figurin' on leavin', so somethin' had to done 'bout it.

"This thing had been goin' on for three or four days. I hadn't minded it myself, 'cause it was sort o' vacation for me. Don't reckon I said more'n a dozen words durin' that time. Windy was what the crowd had named this great hunter, an' that's what we'll call him. It wouldn't be fair to call him by his right name. Well, it was gittin' a bit late one evenin' when Windy makes a mistake. He asks if I'd ever hunted big game.

"'Nothin' bigger'n buffalo,' I says. 'Used to hunt them fellers when I was a young sprout.'

"'Now that's my one great regret,' Windy says. 'I would have given half my fortune for the pleasure of hunting the buffalo.'

"'Well,' say I, 'I don't reckon you'd got much pleasure out o' it. Huntin' lions and tigers ain't nothin' like huntin' buffalo. Them critters traveled in herds, an' a feller's life shore wasn't worth much if he chanced to git in the way o' a stampede. I was ketched in one myself onct.'

"I stops to roll a cigarette, an' Windy was all set to jump in. Reckon he had a mind to argue the point, but the folks didn't give him no chance. They yells for me to tell 'em about the stampede. 'Well, folks,' I says, 'I wasn't actually huntin' nothin' at the time. I was doin' a little scoutin' for the army when that herd o' buffalo cut across my trail.

"'I was headin' north along a narrow canyon. It was 'bout a hundred feet deep, an' I was lookin' for a way to git across. Sudden like, I seen a cloud o' dust rollin' up over the mesa east o' me. Then come a roarin' sound, like thunder. I knowed what it was all right, an' I knowed I was in a fix too. I had a good hoss under me, an' any other time it would've been good sport. But Pinto just wasn't fit for no racin' that day. He'd stepped into a gopher hole the day before an' stoved a front leg. I knowed a couple o' hundred pounds was too much for him on that lame leg, an' he was too good a hoss to throw away.

"'Now it's takin' me ten times as long to tell 'bout it as it did to do what little thinkin' was called for. I jumps off Pinto just as them buffalo come pourin' over the mesa. I'm tellin' you, it looked like the Mississippi River when it busts through a levee. Well, in half a minute I had the saddle off Pinto, an' it shore didn't need no urgin' to git him on his way. Then I unhitches my carbine, an' throws myself behind the saddle.

"'It seemed like I waited a long time, but it shore couldn't have been more'n a few seconds. When there wasn't but 'bout thirty feet 'tween me an' them bellerin' critters, I begun firin'. A dozen o' 'em went down in half that many seconds. They piled up there in front o' me like a stone wall. An' I just had time to crawl up beside a big bull when the flood come pourin' over that wall.

"' 'Course, them buffalo had seen me an' they was so ragin' mad they plumb forgot 'bout the canyon. Into that yawnin' ditch they went, bellerin' an' roarin' like fiends out o' hell.

"'Well, I must've laid there an hour 'fore the last o' them critters disappeared. Then I stretched myself an' went to have me a look at the canyon. But I'm tellin' you, folks, there wasn't no canyon. If I'd been minded, I could've walked across on the backs o' them dead buffalos. Seein' he wasn't in no danger, Pinto had stopped to watch the show 'bout a mile off. I whistled for him. An' knowin' the army was powerful short o' meat right then, I rode into the fort that night to give the report. I heard afterward that the army had estimated as how there was nigh onto fifty thousand head in that herd o' buffalo.' "

"What did the big-game hunter have to say to that?" someone asked, when Jim had finished.

"Nothin'," he drawled. "Must've thought o' somethin' important though. Anyways, he didn't lose no time gittin' to his cabin. He'd booked his passage with us for a month, but he packed up an' left the next day."

Beyond Question

It was the day after Jim Dawson had told the dudes about the buffalo stampede that one of them raised a question concerning it.

"Mr. Dawson," she said, "that was a very interesting story you told us last night. But I've been wondering if it was an actual experience, or just something you thought up for the occasion?" Jim gazed at the speaker through half-closed eyes, as though he too was wondering–wondering whether or not he should answer the question.

"Well, miss," he finally said, "Jim Dawson's honesty ain't often questioned. But he never gits upset when it is. Nope, he just does what he can to put folks straight. So I reckon I'd best answer you the way my old friend Foxear answered me onct when I was minded to doubt him." Jim rolled a cigarette with the usual deliberation, while the dudes patiently waited.

"Old Foxear," he finally began, "was quite a character.

Don't know if he's still livin' or not; I ain't seen him in quite a spell now. He was a powerful big Injun with a ragged scar on one side o' his face. He claimed it was a birthmark. It was sort o' yellow like, an' always reminded me of a streak o' lightnin'. I asks him one time how he come by it.

"No I don't reckon I can give you his exact words, 'cause it was a long time back, but I'll do the best I can. 'That,' he says to me, 'is mark of great people, my people. Red man once live way off, many suns to east. One day great storm come. Big wind pick up many people, carry 'em up to clouds. Red men travel on clouds many suns over big waters. Clouds break up over new land. People come down. Some come on rain, they sometime called Rain-in-face. Some come on lightning.'

"Foxy looks at me queer like, then touches the mark on his face an' says, 'Lightning mark of great people, my people all medicine men.'

"Then I says to him, 'Look here, Foxy, that's a mighty interestin' tale, but how do I know it's straight?' Well, the old boy just looks up at the sky an' points a long finger at the sun. Then he fires this question at me: 'You sure he is sun?'

"Well, folks, I had to admit it was the sun all right. An' I never questioned the old boy agin."

Allergic to Yellow

Jim Dawson was having a little difficulty in getting the old guitar properly tuned this evening. Taking advantage of the opportunity, one of the dudes said, "Jim, I suppose you've never had any trouble with the women guests."

"Not much," was the guarded reply.

"But some," the dude persisted.

"Well," Jim drawled, "I wouldn't say as how it was trouble. More apt to be amusin'."

"Couldn't you favor us with one such experience?"

"Reckon I could," Jim replied, "but the ladies might not enjoy it."

Being assure, however, that those present would enjoy it, Jim laid the guitar aside. He proceeded with the making of a cigarette as he began his story.

"There was a lady drifted in her from Californy one time," he said. "She wasn't young an' she wasn't nowise much to look at. But, from the way she strutted 'round here, she must've been used to havin' her own way most o' the time. Nothing' ever pleased her. She had the whole place upset in a couple o' days–all except me. She didn't brother me much. I just humored her, you might say."

"What would she do?" someone asked, as Jim paused to light the cigarette.

"Oh, she never liked the hosses I give her," he continued. "First one was too slow, next one too fast. She tried a dozen saddles 'fore she got one to her likin'. Then we wouldn't no more'n git started till I'd have to fix one o' her stirrups. Mebbe we'd make half a mile 'for the other one had to be fixed different.

"That had been going for three or for days. An', as I told you, it wasn't botherin' me much, but I could see the rest o' the folks was gittin' squirmy. Well, she comes out one mornin' wearing' a bright yeller shirt. She was shore strong on bright colors, that gal was, never wearin' the same shirt twict. She rode Flossy the day before an' hadn't' found much to complain about. Now Flossy was gittin' 'long in years too, but she was still a good hoss. Leastwise, she had a good disposition.

"Course I had Flossy ready for her that mornin'. We'd been waitin' most nigh an hour, an' mebbe I was gittin' a bit itchy myself. The gal with the shirts was never on time. Anyways, when I seen that yeller shirt, I pulls the saddle off Flossy. I was just leadin' the hoss away when she comes up to me. 'Sorry, mam,' I says, 'but you can't ride Flossy this mornin'.' She looks at me sharp like, an' says, 'An' why not?'

"'On account it ain't safe,' I says. 'Flossy don't like yeller.' If you was to git on her with that shirt, she'd more'n likely run off with you. I'll git another hoss.' Now we had a big burro we called Flicker. We give him that name 'cause he was always flickin' his long ears. He was always hangin' 'round the barn, so I didn't have no trouble findin' him.

"'Do you expect me to ride that beast?' the gal exploded, when she seen Flicker. 'There ain't no choice now,' I says. 'Flicker's all that's left. I'm sorry mam.' But my regrets didn't do no good. That gal just throwed her head back like a scared colt an' went snortin' off to her cabin. I couldn't figure why everybody was lookin' so happy that evenin' till I found out the gal from Californy had took off that afternoon."

"That was a very clever stunt, Jim," one of the dudes remarked.

"Don't reckon as how I'm follerin' yorr," Jim returned.

"Why, you know horses aren't allergic to colors."

"Ain't which?"

"Allergic–sensitive. Horses are not affected by color."

"There you go, doubtin' Jim Dawson's honesty agin." Jim's lazy eyes assumed an expression of injury as he picked up the guitar.

"No," the dude returned, "I don't mean to question your honesty, Jim. I'm only doubting that your horse Flossy even noticed the lady's shirt."

"She shore did," Jim replied. "Flossy seen it all right. An' she shore would've been hoppin' mad if that gal had got on her."

"But why?" someone asked.

"Well," Jim explained, "Flossy was scared onct when she was young an' she didn't never get over it. She was a four-year-old when one o' them candy cowpokes from Hollywood come out here. He wants to ride a young hoss with plenty o' spirit, so I picks out Flossy for him. He was wearin' a heap o' fancy gear, includin' a yeller shirt an' a pair o' them cute little Mexican spurs.

"Now I hadn't noticed them spurs, else the thing wouldn't never happened. Well, Mr. Movie King he hops onto Flossy an' digs them spurs in her ribs. Wanted to show us how good he was, I reckon. Anyways, that was somethin' new to Flossy, an' she shore put on a show.

"When we digs that feller out o' the dust a couple o' minutes later," Jim concluded, "I don't reckon his own mother would've knowed him. He wasn't hurt much, 'cept a busted arm. The next day he went to look for someplace where the ground was softer."

"But I don't see what the yellow shirt had to do with it," said one of the dudes.

"It didn't have nothin' to do with it in the beginnin'," Jim replied. "But, you see, after that Flossy never seen yeller without thinkin' o' spurs. An' she didn't have no more likin' for them things than a cat has for mustard."

Not Much Help

A famous astrologer spent a month at the Lazy R one summer. As the days passed she became very much interested in the head wrangler.

"Mr. Dawson," she said to him one day, "I would like very much to know the hour and the date of your birth. It would be interesting to learn what astrological influences had been responsible for such an unusual character."

From some of the discussions he had already heard Jim

knew that astrology had something to do with science. Being suspicious of anything connected with science, he looked warily at the questioner before attempting an answer.

"I'm sorry, mam," he finally said, "but I can't give you no exact figures relatin' to the time I was hatched."

"Now," the lady exclaimed, "you surely know when you were born!"

"Yep," he returned, with his usual indifference, "I know 'bout when it was, all right."

"But I thought you said you didn't know."

"Nope, you got me wrong," Jim drawled. "I said as how I couldn't give you no figures." Obviously, the lady was somewhat puzzled, as well as annoyed.

"That's unfortunate," she said, "for I would have enjoyed forecasting your future."

"Well," he replied, as a smile played about his mouth, "if the information's worth anythin' to you, I can tell you I come to life the night the new moon follered the second Sunday in April."

"That's rather indefinite," she returned, somewhat dis gustedly.

"Yep," Jim replied, "I reckon it is. But you see, mam, we didn't have no calendars in them days, an' no clocks neither. I don't seem to have much recollection o' the occasion myself, but I've heard my mother tell 'bout it. She said she heard a rooster crowin' just 'bout the time I let out my first squawk. That would've been 'bout an hour 'fore sunup. An' she said she re membered seein' the new moon 'fore she went to bed that night."

"How did she know it was the second Sunday in the month?" the astrologer inquired.

"Well, you see, mam," Jim drawled, "it wasn't no chore to keep track o' Sundays in them days. We lived in the country, an' that was the only day in the week we ever had company."

Well Named

The horses were being rested after a long climb. Jim Dawson sat on his boot heels tracing meaningless designs on the hard ground with a burned match.

"Jim," one of the dudes said, "I've often heard you speak of the Indian Foxear. Did you ever learn how he came to have such an odd name?" Jim pushed the weathered sombrero farther back on his head.

"Nope," he replied. "You see, Injuns don't like to talk 'bout their names. But I reckon he got that name on account o' his hearin'. The old boy shore had a pair o' sharp ears.

"One day he drifted in here out o' nowheres an' asks for the Boss. It turns out he wants to swap a pocketful o' turquoise for a hoss. Well, him an' the Boss went down to the corral, an' they was there most o' the afternoon wranglin' over the deal an' gittin' nowheres. It was gittin' nigh onto suppertime, when all o' a sudden old Foxy's head comes up like somebody'd slapped him under his chin. He stands there a minute lookin' off into the southwest. Don't reckon you could actually call it lookin' though, 'cause his eyes was most nigh shut. But his head was cocked to one side, like he was listenin' for somethin'.

"Now we hadn't had no rain in 'bout six months, an' there hadn't been a cloud in the sky for weeks. All at onct Foxy straightens up, an' he says, 'Big storm come. Me hear thunder.' I had right good ears myself, but I shore didn't hear nothin'. Well, the old boy raises the ante on the hoss, an' the Boss calls him. Then he hitches a hackamoor on the hoss an' hops on his back like I used to do when I was a kid. In less time than it takes to tell it, he'd disappeared in a cloud o' dust, an' we didn't see him agin for a whole year."

"How about the storm?" someone asked.

"We got the storm all right," Jim drawled. "An' she shore was a humdinger."

"I suppose it began to rain almost before the Indian was out of sight," someone else suggested, derisively.

"Nope," Jim replied, "it was two days 'fore that storm hit here."

A Plausible Explanation

The dudes had eaten lunch in the shade of a wind twisted juniper high up on the mesa today. Now they were sprawled out in comfortable relaxation, the new arrivals in speechless admiration of the vast panorama which stretched for miles and miles before them until lost in the misty distance.

"I wonder what kind of a bird that is?" someone asked, gazing skyward.

The question prompted considerable speculation but no agreement, as all eyes were centered upon the big bird which floated lazily through the cloudless sky.

"Jim," one of the party remarked, "it looks as though you would have to settle the argument. What's that bird up there? I say it's a buzzard."

Jim Dawson had just finished packing away the lunch equipment. He strolled up to the edge of the group, gazed into the sky with squinting eyes, and answered, "Nope, that ain't no buzzard. Buzzards don't travel that high. That's an eagle."

"An eagle!" one of the gentlemen exclaimed; suddenly

sitting up, as though to get a better view of the soaring bird. "Why, I didn't know you had eagles in this part" of the country."

"Yep," Jim drawled, easing his long frame onto his boot heels. "Yep, we got most everything out here–even to eagles," he added with a lazy grin.

"But not the bald variety," the noted professor quickly returned.

"Yep, the very same," Jim corrected, leisurely rolling a cigarette. "There's lots of 'em back in the mountains."

"I've seen those big birds in the zoo," one of the feminine members remarked, "and I've always wondered why they were baldheaded."

That casual remark started another discussion, the learned professor attempting to explain the phenomenon. It was easy to see, however, that his scientific explanation was not entirely satisfactory to his audience.

Finally, one of the guests who knew Jim Dawson from past experience turned to the old cowhand. "Jim," he said, with a knowing smile, "what do you think regarding this question?"

"Well," Jim drawled, "I ain't sayin' the professor couldn't be right, 'cause I ain't never been acquainted with science. All I can say is that it ain't accordin' to the story I heard."

"What was the story you heard, Jim? Tell us about it."

A reminiscent smile played about Jim Dawson's generous mouth, as he gazed again at the bird which was now but a speck on the horizon.

"Oh, it ain't much o' a story," he began. "But it seemed reasonable 'nuff the first time I heard it, an' I ain't never had no cause to change my mind. I got the story from my dad when I was a little feller. Now, you see, my dad hadn't never been to college, but he was right smart just the same."

Jim took time out to roll another cigarette before launching upon his tale. "Now accordin' to the story as I got it," he finally said, "them eagles wasn't always baldheaded. In the beginnin' they had feathers on their heads like all the other birds. The trouble goes back to the time o' the big flood.

"You see, when Noah was packing the animals an' birds into the ark, Mr. and Mrs. Eagle was sailin' around through the sun shine 'way above the clouds. They didn't know the water was gittin' so high down on the old earth. An' when they decided it was time to eat, they sailed down through the clouds an' dis covered there wasn't no place to land 'cept on top o' the ark.

"By that time the ark was already floatin' off on the muddy water. But when Noah seen them birds, he opens the door an' invites 'em in. Well, Mr. an' Mrs. Eagle went into a huddle an' decided they better take a chance. But they hadn't been inside that place long 'fore they was shore they'd made a mistake. It was so crowded there wasn't no place for them poor birds to roost 'cept on a crossbar 'way up under the roof.

"Now them eagles wasn't used to livin' in such tight quarters, an' you can shore bet they wasn't no ways happy. So when the ark finally landed on solid ground an' the doors was opened, they didn't lose no time gittin' out o' that old coop. They flew up into the sky an' played in the good old sunshine like a couple o' kids."

Jim Dawson gave his audience a slow smile as he began to roll another cigarette. Apparently the story was ended, to the disappointment of his listeners.

"But, Jim," someone protested, "what does all that have to do with the eagles' bald heads?"

'Tm comin' to that," Jim drawled, striking a match with his thumbnail. "Now when them birds gits tired frolickin' in the sky, they comes down an' lands on a dead tree. They sits there a long time just lookin' at each other. After a while Mrs. Eagle begun to laugh.

"What's the joke," says Mr. Eagle.

"You," says she. "You're the funniest-lookin' thing I ever seen. You ain't got a single feather on your head." .

"Well," snapped her lord and master, "you ain't got no call to be laughin' 'bout it. Your own head looks like a hen's egg."

"You see, folks, them days in the ark had been so rough, with the old crate bobbin' like a cork in a teakettle, that them birds had scraped their heads against the roof till there wasn't no feathers left on 'em. But that wasn't the worst of it. Them feathers never growed back agin."

"Is that all of the story?" someone asked.

"That's all my dad ever told me," Jim replied. "But it ain't hard to guess the rest. Like as not, them birds begun lookin' for the highest mountain they could find. Anyways, that's where they've always lived. Reckon they're so 'shamed o' their bald heads that they don't want no one to see 'em. A tough break, I calls it."

Well Advised

"Mr. Dawson, what were those queer-looking animals we saw down in the meadow as we came in this afternoon?"

Jim Dawson had taken his usual place on the veranda steps this evening. He was having difficulty getting his old guitar tuned to his liking.

"Them was jack rabbits, miss," Jim replied, without looking up.

"Oh! Jack rabbits! I never saw one before. Curious animals, aren't they?"

"Well, I don't know about that," was the drawling answer. "With them big ears, they ought to be plenty generous. But curious? Well, I ain't never heard of 'em bein' very curious."

"But that wasn't what I meant," she returned. "I meant that they were so queer looking, with those big ears and long

legs. Is there any reason why they should have such long legs?"

"Plenty," Jim said, laying the guitar aside to roll a cigarette. "It ain't likely they'd be here if it wasn't for them legs."

"How's that, Jim?" someone asked. "Tell us about it." "Well," Jim drawled, "I'll give it to you just as I got it from my old friend Foxear. He claims he got it straight, so I reckon we've got to take his word for it. Old Foxear says it all started 'bout the time his people first come to this country. There was lots o' rabbits here then, he says, but it wasn't long till they begun to git scarce.

"Now that bothered them Injuns, 'cause they was right fond o' rabbit stew. An' it wasn't the Injuns that was killin' off the rabbits. They never killed more game than they needed, anyways.

"Well, one night the old Medicine Man was sittin' beside the river watchin' the moonbeams dancin' on the water, when a big buck rabbit hops up an' sits down beside him. The old man knows this is the chief o' the rabbit clan; he seen the marks on his ear.

"Well, chief rabbit told his troubles to the Medicine Man, an' they talked an' talked till the moon went down. The old man found out that the reason the rabbits was gittin' scarce was 'cause the coyotes was killin' 'em off faster'n they could breed. So when chief rabbit got home the next morn in ', the first thing he done was to call a meetin' o' the council. He told 'em what the Medicine Man had said, an' they agreed it was a good idea. They adjourned the meetin' an' went scamperin' off to spread the good news. You see, the old Injun had told chief rabbit that the only way to lick the coyotes was to grow longer legs so they could run faster."

Jim began to roll a cigarette, but his audience sensed that he had not finished his story. But when he picked up the guitar, it looked very much as though they had been mistaken.

"But, Jim," someone asked, "how does it come that the cottontails still have short legs? Don't they both belong to the same family?"

"Shore," Jim returned. "But, you see, them crazy rabbits wasn't all agreed that the old Injun's advice was any good. I reckon some of 'em was just too lazy to try it–like a lot o' humans. Anyways, them that did try it soon growed legs long 'nuff to outrun the coyotes. Them's the ones we call jack rabbits now, but they ought've been named Progressives. Them that was satisfied with their short legs is called cottontails, but the fact is, Conservatives would be a better name for 'em."

"Jim," one of the guests remarked, when the story appeared to be closed, "that was a great tale, but it seems to me that it had a bad flaw in it."

"Think so?" Jim returned, quietly thrumming his guitar. "Yes, I do, because it doesn't explain how the cottontails managed to survive."

Jim Dawson scratched his head a moment before starting the manufacture of another cigarette. "Well," he finally drawled, "that ain't so hard to savvy when you know all the facts. There wouldn't be no cottontails if the jack rabbits hadn't discouraged the coyotes." Again Jim paused.

"But how were they discouraged, Jim?"

"Well you see, the old Injun give the rabbit some good ad vice on how to use them long legs after they'd growed 'em. An' it shore worked too. You see, when a coyote takes after a jack rabbit, that old boy puts full steam back o' them long legs till he locates a good-sized cactus or a bush o' cat's-claw. Then he slows down an' lets Mr. Coyote git closer to him. 'Course the coyote thinks it's all over now, an' he starts lickin' his chops an' not payin' much attention to where he's goin'.

"An' when Mr. Coyote figures it's 'bout time to gather in his dinner, he sees the jack rabbit leap right over the top o' that murderous bush, an' he hits it head on.

"Well," Jim concluded, with a satisfied grin, "you can· see for yourselves how it would be. When Mr. Coyote gits himself untangled, with his head full o' stickers, he's sort o' lost his appetite for rabbit."

An Old Debt

Jim Dawson was proving somewhat disappointing this evening. Several guests had tried to lead him into the telling of a story, but without success. Jim had been generous enough with his quaint songs, but had tactfully detoured around all questions calculated to draw him out.

Finally someone asked, "Jim, what would you do if you had a million dollars?"

Jim looked at the questioner with half-closed eyes for a long moment before he replied.

"A which?" he asked.

"A million dollars—all money."

"You expectin' an' honest answer?" Jim returned. "Yes, of course."

"Humph! A million dollars," Jim muttered, as though talking to himself. "Nobody with the brains o' a chipmunk would want that much money."

"But lots of people have more than that, Jim," the guest persisted. "And some of them are supposed to be quite smart too."

"So I've heard," Jim returned, "an' I'm right glad I ain't one o' 'em."

"But you haven't yet answered the question. If you had that much money, what would you do with it?" "Git shed of it pronto," was the quick retort.

"But think of the good time you could have, Jim," someone remarked. "You wouldn't have to work any more."

"Well, miss," Jim drawled, 'Tm thinkin' that's where

you're wrong. From what I've heard concernin' big money, I reckon if I had a million dollars I'd be workin' a durned sight harder'n I do now."

"Then you would rather be a wrangler than a million-aire?" "Lots more fun," Jim stoutly declared.

"Well, you're the first person I ever heard say they would rather work than play."

"It ain't work when you're doin' what you like to do." "Well anyway, you said if a million dollars did come your way, you would get rid of it in a hurry. Now just how would you go about doing that?"

"Easy 'nuff," was the drawling reply. "I'd keep out four or five thousand, pack up the rest o' the stuff, an' ship it back where it come from."

"Then you would keep a little of it for yourself."

"I ain't said so." Jim hesitated, as though reluctant to pursue the subject further. "Well, whatever I kept out o' that pile o' trouble I'd give to Molly Henderson."

"Ohl" The rising inflection attached to that exclamation was silently echoed by most of those present. "A girl friend?" "A friend," was Jim's tardy reply. "But you couldn't hardly call her a girl, seein' as how she's most nigh old 'nuff to be my mother." That statement had silenced his audience, and Jim now picked up the old guitar, indicating that the subject was closed.

The Boss now spoke. He had joined the group at the opening of this discussion. "Jim," he said, "I imagine the folks would like to hear about the incident that was responsible for your friendship with Molly Henderson. Would you mind telling them about it?"

"No, I reckon not." Jim's response had come somewhat reluctantly, as he began to roll a cigarette.

"Molly was runnin' a boardin' house when I first come into this country," he finally began. "My first job was fifty miles from town, so we didn't git in too often. When we did go in, we generally hung 'round for a couple o' days. I always stayed at Molly Henderson's, 'cause her cookin' was the best in town. I got to know Molly right well. I liked her 'cause she was as game as they come. Her man had been killed in a gun battle, but that didn't stop Molly.

"Well, one night when I was in town with a couple o' months' pay in my pocket, I drops into the Silver Star to see how my luck was runnin'. I hadn't been sittin' in the game long 'fore I caught the dealer slippin' a card. I calls him an' he blows up. When he reaches for his six-shooter, I wings him pronto. A feller ain't smart, tryin' that stuff if he ain't mighty fast on the draw.

"Well, when the smoke clears away I figures I might as well call it a day. So I ambles up to Molly's an' hits the hay. When I come to next mornin', the sun was shinin' into the room full blast. I was arguin' with myself whether to crawl out or take another turn, when there's a poundin' on the front door.

"In a minute I hears Molly sayin', "Good mornin', sheriff!" I couldn't hear what the sheriff said, but it didn't matter none. I heard Molly sayin', 'No, sheriff, Jim Dawson ain't here, an' I ain't seen him for months.' Then I heard the sheriff stompin' down the steps. In a minute there was a knock on my door, an' Molly was whisperin', 'Jim! Jim, are you awake?'"

"Well, I was most nigh dressed by that time, so I opens the door. Molly says to me, 'Son,' she says, 'you git yourself onto that broom-tail o' yours an' git goin' 'fore the sheriff finds out I lied to him.' 'I'm on my way, Molly,' I says, puttin' on my shirt while I'm follerin' her to the kitchen.

"I was goin' out the door when she sticks a cup o' hot coffee under my nose, sayin', 'Put this inside your shirt, you'll be needin' it 'fore you gits home.' She stuffs some biscuits into my pocket while I'm gulpin' the coffee. 'Now hit the trail,' she says, 'an' you needn't be in no hurry comin' back. You better be keepin' under cover till this thing's blowed over.' "

"Well, it was six months 'fore I seen the town again, an' then I sneaked in after dark. I didn't unsaddle, just turned my hoss loose in the corral, figurin' I might need him in a hurry. You see, I wasn't takin' no chances. Molly was in the kitchen when I stuck my head in the door. She was washin' dishes an' hadn't heard me slippin' up on the porch.

"'How about it, Molly?' I says. An' she just looks 'round at me like she'd seen me that mornin'. She don't say a word while she's dryin' her hands, just looks at me queer like. Then she busts out laughin'. Now I couldn't figure where the joke was, but, havin' no call to be gittin' sore at Molly Henderson, I waits till she sobers up. Then I says, 'Is it safe to come in?' 'Shore,' she says. 'Sit yourself while I git you somethin' to eat. You look like you ain't had a good meal since I last seen you.' She laughs agin, sayin', 'An' that's a right smart while. You could've come back the next week.'

"'What do you mean?' I asks. 'Well,' she says, 'the sheriff found out that bird you winged in the Silver Star was wanted in Texas for horse-stealin'. You can bet they didn't lose no time shippin' him down there.'

"'Damn funny,' I says, 'that nobody never told ME 'bout it.' 'Yes,' says Molly, keepin' her eyes on the stove, where she's fryin' me a skillet full o' eggs. 'Yes, it is right funny, isn't it?'

"Well," Jim concluded, "it was a long time 'fore it go through my thick noodle that it was Molly's way o' keepin' me out o' trouble for a little while." He picked up the guitar, adding almost inaudibly, "Good old Molly." He stood erect, gazing up at the stars for a moment. Then he took a long breath, as he said, "Well, good night, folks," and disappeared in the darkness.

Culling All Inventors

One summer there came to the Lazy R ranch an outstanding figure in the field of aeronautics. He was a very pompous, very talkative, self-opinionated person, decidedly annoying to the guests at times.

His first encounter with Jim Dawson was down at the corral, the morning after his arrival. Jim was fitting a new shoe on one of the horses. He swiftly appraised the stranger out of the corner of his eye, without apparent interruption of his work. "Mornin'," he drawled.

"Good morning," was the tardy response, as the big man surveyed this oddity of the human species. Then, with great dignity, he introduced himself. "My name is Bush; J. Larimore Bush. You've heard of me, of course. I'm research engineer for–"

"Re-which?" Jim inquired, straightening up to inspect the stranger more closely.

"Re-which?" Jim inquired, straightening up to inspect the stranger more closely.

"Research, my man–research," snapped J. Larimore Bush.

"Humpf!" came from Jim, as he returned to his task. "Don't reckon I know a poorer place for searchin'. Ain't nothin' been found 'round here in the last hundred years."

J. Larimore glared at Jim's broad back for a long moment before taking his not so dignified departure. He was considerably nettled over his failure to impress this crude individual in boots and jeans.

Two weeks passed. And during that time the guests found little pleasure in the presence of J. Larimore Bush, except his ineffectual efforts to involve Jim Dawson in a discussion of his pet subject. Apparently, the famous engineer believed that there was only one subject worthy of conversation and that was aeronautics. And it was also evident that, in his opinion at least, there was no one quite as well posted on that subject as himself. In his august opinion, it would be only a short time until the air would provide the one means of transportation. He could even see the day, not far off, when horses would no longer be used on dude ranches; miniature airplanes would eventually supplant these plodding animals.

No one who knew him could remember Jim Dawson ever having maintained such glum silence. Stranger than that, however, was the fact that Jim had failed to take his accustomed place on the veranda steps the previous evening. Nor had he appeared tonight. The guests did not know, of course, that the Boss was now on his way to Jim's cabin. He too was concerned about his trusted foreman. He found Jim sitting in the doorway with his head in his hands.

"Why, Jim," he exclaimed, "you aren't sick, are you?" Without looking up, Jim replied, "Yep, I shore am." "What's wrong; what is it, old man?" Jim looked at his friend with a helpless expression in his lazy eyes. "What is it?" the Boss repeated.

"J. Larimore Bush," was the laconic reply. "I've had airnotics pounded into my ears till I reckon I've got airitis."

"Not much wonder," the Boss returned. "If that man stays here much longer, we'll all be nuts." At that Jim scrambled to his feet and disappeared within the cabin. When he reappeared he had his guitar under his arm. As he started for the ranch house, he said, "You might let a feller know how you feel about these things."

Jim's welcome was most enthusiastic, as he took his customary seat and began to tune the old guitar. He made several attempts to entertain the guests with song and music, but with little success. J. Larimore Bush never ceased his monotonous chatter.

Jim had finally given up and was now sitting with his elbows on the guitar in his lap, gazing listlessly up at the stars. The famous engineer had just launched upon the subject of gravity. Suddenly his voice trailed off, while his beady eyes rested upon Jim Dawson. Then he leaned far forward in his chair.

"Perhaps," he said, "our friend Mr. Dawson could tell us something about gravity if he would."

Slowly shifting his gaze to the speaker, Jim replied, "Which one?"

Which one?" The pompous J. Larimore laughed unpleasantly. "Why, man, don't you know there's only one gravity?" There had been an unmistakable sneer in that sharp reply.

"That ain't accordin' to my calendar," was Jim's calm reply.

"What do you mean?" the big man demanded, with evident annoyance.

"Well," Jim drawled, preparing to roll a cigarette, "I ain't never laid claim to knowin' much, but I shore know one thing; there's two kinds o' gravity, an' I thought everybody knowed that."

"And what do you think they are?" snapped J. Larimore Bush.

"Well," Jim returned, "mebbe I'll have some trouble makin' it plain, but I'll do the best I can." He carefully finished the cigarette before continuing. "Now I reckon the kind o' gravity you're best acquainted with is the one that Nature made. She put that thing here to keep us from slippin' off the globe as it goes spinnin' round the sun. The other kind o' gravity was invented by man, I reckon, anyways; it's what keeps us from laughin' when somethin' happens that ain't no joke."

"Absurd" came from J. Larimore Bush, in a harsh undertone.

"An' I reckon," Jim continued, as though he had not heard, "yep, I reckon it might not be a bad thing if we had another kind o' gravity, or somethin' along that line. Mighty funny somebody ain't invented it long 'fore this. You see,

Mother Nature does a right good job o' keepin' our feet on the ground, but it looks to me like we needed somethin' that would work on the head too."

"What do you mean, Jim?" someone hastened to inquire. Jim Dawson had tucked the guitar under his arm and was already going down the steps. He stopped, looking back with narrowed eyes.

"Well," he drawled, "I've always thought it might save some folks a lot o' sufferin' if there was somethin' to let the pressure off their heads. It must be mighty painful when a feller's head gits so big it's most ready to bust."

"Thanks, Jim," said the Boss next morning. He was getting the car ready to take J. Larimore Bush to town.

Foxear the Trader

The guests were resting in the shadow of Rambler Mountain before returning to the ranch. One of the guests had been watching Jim Dawson with decided interest, as he rolled a cigarette.

"Mr. Dawson," she finally said, "I hope you don't mind my admiring that ring you're wearing. It's one of the loveliest of the kind that I've ever seen." Jim merely smiled, as he took off the ring and handed it to the young lady.

"Oh, it's lovely!" she exclaimed. "And it looks as though it might be very old. Have you had it a long time?"

"Nope," Jim returned. "I only got it a few years back."

"You must have put out a goodly sum for it," she remarked, returning the heavy ring with evident reluctance."

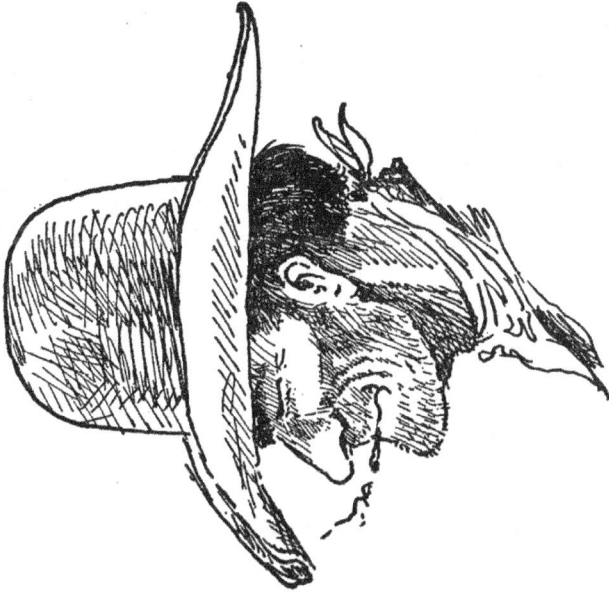

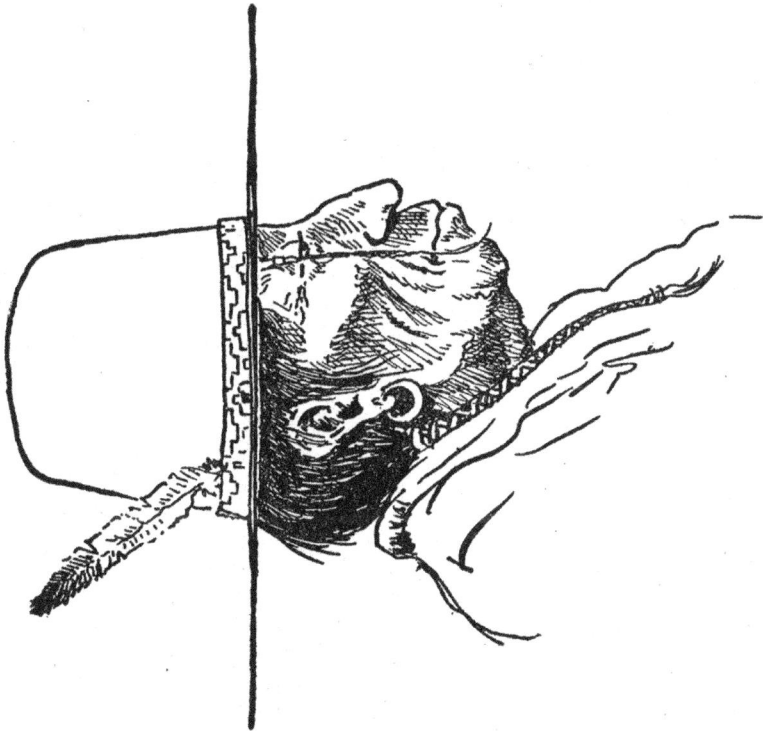

Nope," Jim replied, with a reminiscent grin. "It didn't cost me nothin'."

"A wonderful gift, I would say."

"Well, it wasn't exactly a gift. You see, I got it in a trade."

"Tell us about it, Jim," someone requested, as Jim slipped the ring back on his long finger.

"Oh, there ain't much to tell," Jim drawled. "Sort o' funny though, how it come about. You see, I'm the only one on the ranch durin' the winter. An' when a feller lives alone he ain't likely to pay much heed to time. Well, the snow was 'bout gone, an' it looked like spring wasn't too far oft. So I rode to town one day; sort o' wonderin' what the world was doin', you know. I was packin' a sack o' mail on my way back, for, you see, I ain't been to town in more'n four months." Jim stopped to roll another cigarette.

"When I got home," he finally continued, "there was old Foxear toastin' his shins in my cabin. I was right glad to see the old boy, 'cause he hadn't been 'round for a long time. Well, I dumped the mail on the table, wonderin' if there might be somethin' for me.

"Yep, there was a letter from the Boss in California, besides a couple o' Christmas cards an' a package for me. Well, I opened the package an' found it was from one of our old guests in the East. He had sent me a couple o' decks o' fancy playin' cards an' a box o' chips. It was gittin' dark, so I left the stuff on the table an' went out to do the chores.

"Well, when I got back to the cabin, there was old Foxear fingerin' them colored chips like they was nuggets o' gold. He holds up one, an' says, 'You want?'

"Well, I shore hadn't no need for 'em, but I says, .Oh, I don't know. Do you want 'em?' Foxy sits there lookin, at them things a long time. Then he puts his hands 'round the pile, an' says, 'How much?'

"'Now, let's see,' I says, an' begun stackin' 'em. Twenty blues,' I says, 'worth a dollar each; twenty reds, at four bits each; twenty whites, at two bits. Let's see, that's twenty, an' ten, an' five. They might be worth thirty-five Foxear,' I says. The old boy was so busy watchin' them stacks o' colored bone that he didn't notice me grinnin' at him.

"Well, I had supper cooked an' was clearin' off the table. Foxear hadn't said a word, just sat there lookin' at them things like he was in a dream. All of a sudden he pulls this ring off his finger an' holds it out to me, coverin' the chips with his other hand. 'Me trade,' he says.

"I looks at the ring, then at Foxear, wonderin' what the old boy was up to. Then, figurin' he must be jokin', I says, 'This thing ain't worth thirty-five dollars. But if you want them things that bad, they're yours, Foxy.' Foxear just grins an' starts stuffin' them chips inside his shirt. It looked like he thought he'd made a good deal. An' I didn't find out till late that summer that I'd got the worst o' it."

"How was that, Jim," someone asked. "It looks to me as though that ring should buy a truckload of poker chips."

"An' that's what I thought," Jim slowly replied. "But I was dead wrong. Old Foxy sold them chips for a dollar apiece." When the laughter had subsided, someone asked, "But how could he? Who was simple enough to give a dollar for a poker chip, I would like to know."

"Foxy done it easy 'nuff," Jim returned. "He took them chips home an' put shiny copper bands 'round 'em. Then he made 'em into two belts. He sold them red, white, an' blue belts to one o' the dudes for sixty dollars."

An Unfortunate Handicap

It was a beautiful night. The wind had gone to rest from a hard day's labor, and the stars were dazzling in their seeming nearness. Jim Dawson had just finished singing "Boots and Saddles."

"Jim," one of the guests remarked, "you should be on the radio." Jim only smiled, as he extracted the Bull Durham from his shirt pocket.

"That's right!" a newcomer enthusiastically agreed, "I've never heard that song done half so well on the radio. And you certainly get the best our of that guitar."

"Well, miss," Jim returned, with a smile, "I don't reckon I'm much to blame for that. You see, I've had this music box a long, long time. It hadn't never been worked on when I got it. I sort o' brung it up, you might say. An' we've worked together so long now that the old boy performs right well without much promptin' from me."

"You're much too modest, Jim," someone interposed. "But seriously, have you never thought of making better use of your talent?" Jim made no response, so the guest added, "You know, there's good money in the entertainment field."

"So I've heard," Jim drawled, as he lit the cigarette. "Nope, I ain't hankerin' after no sich life. No hoss to ride, an' if I stayed in one o' them big cities six months I'd be plumb locoed." He picked up the guitar again, adding, "I had a chance at the show business onct."

"Please tell us about it, Jim," one of the guests urged. The long fingers moved idly over the tuneful strings, while Jim gazed skyward. Then he chuckled.

"Right funny, how it come about," he drawled. "It was down in Texas, the winter 'fore I come up to this country. Bein' in town one day, an' not havin' much to do, I drops into the Palace to see if any o' my cronies was hangin' 'round there. A goodly crowd was lined up at the bar, an' a big feller with pointed whiskers was doin' the talkin'.

"I heard him tellin' the crowd that he was willin' to lay a little bet that he could plug a silver dollar nine rimes out o' ten at fifty paces. Then I seen the sheriff poke his big paw into his pants pocket. He pulls our a gold piece an' slaps it on the bar. 'There you are, Colonel,' says the sheriff. 'I'm stakin' twenty dollars on that show.'

"Well, the crowd moves out to the street, an' a silver dollar was stuck on a hitchin' post. I was standin' right close to the big stranger when he pulls his six-shooter. The first shot sent that shinin' dollar spinnin' down the street so fast you could hardly see it. He missed the third shot, but the rest was all clean hits. An' he had ruined six silver dollars while he was winnin' twenty from the sheriff. When it was all over, the stranger looks at me, an' says, 'How was that, young man?'

"'Not bad,' I says, 'but I've seen better.'

"'Oh, you have?' says he.

"'Yep, I know a feller what can do as well as that with the dollar standin' edgeway.'

"'I'd like to see that man,, the big feller says.

"'You're lookin' at him, stranger,' says I. Well, the stranger looks at me, sharp like, for a minute, then he laughs. He holds up the sheriff's gold piece, an' says, 'Now, young man, I'm payin' twenty dollars to see that show.'

"Well, somebody sticks up another silver dollar, with the edge facin' me. I pulls the old trusty that my dad had give me when I was fifteen. I gives the trigger a gentle touch, an' that silver dollar went rollin' down the street for nigh a hundred yards.

"Well, folks, the big feller slaps that gold piece into my hand an' shouts, 'That's, nuff, my friend that's 'nuff! Why, son, you're marvelous, simply marvelous. An' you're just wastin' your time here. You belong in my show. An' I'm makin' you an offer right now. A hundred fifty dollars a month an' all expenses. You'll be a sensation, or my name ain't William.'

"Now I'm standin' there with my mouth hangin' open, wonderin' what I'd done to cause all the fuss. Then the big feller turns to the crowd an' laughs again. 'Can you fancy it, men?' he shouts. 'A few minutes ago I was 'lamentin' the fact that I hadn't found a roughrider for my show in this whole county. An' up pops this marvel with gun.'

"Then he turns to me, an' says, 'What do you say, my boy? Will you join my show?' Show,' I says, a funny feelin' creepin' over me. 'What show?'

"'Why, the greatest show on earth, my boy. None other than Buffalo Bill's Wild West. Oh, I forgot we hadn't been introduced,' he says, sort o' apologetic like. 'I'm Colonel Cody.'

"Well, I'm tellin' you, folks, I felt sort o' limp right then. If Buffalo Bill had bet I couldn't hit the hoss that was standin' across the street, I reckon he would've won. 'Well, what do you say?' I heard him sayin'.

"'Nope,' I says to him, an' I knowed my voice wasn't natural. 'Thanks, Colonel,' I says. 'You'r offer's mighty gratifyin', but I ain't got no business takin' it up.' 'Course he wants to know why, an' I ain't got the nerve to confess the truth.

"Sufferin' tomcats, it give me the creeps just to think 'bout it. I could see myself standin' in a big ring all alone, with thousands o' folks startin' at me. Nope, I knowed mighty well I could never do it. Here, among friends, it wasn't no trick at all–but never in a show, with a crowd o' strangers watchin' me.

"While I was tryin' to find a way out o' the mess I'd got myself into, my eyes lit on the sheriff standin' a few yards off. He was playin' with them silver dollars what Buffalo Bill had shot to pieces. That give me an idea, so I speaks up, more natural like now.

"'I'm mighty sorry I can't go 'long with you, Colonel,' I says. 'But–well, it's like this. You see, my folks is Scotch, an' it would 'bout break my heart if I had to spoil so much good money." '

Solving a Problem

If Jim Dawson over took a dislike to anyone who came to the Lazy R, they never knew it. Jim did his best to treat the guests all alike, regardless of who, or what, they might be.

It was the noted doctor from New York who came the closest to upsetting Jim's customary tranquility. This blustering specialist from the big city spent a month at the ranch one summer. Why he had chosen a dude ranch for his vacation was an unanswerable question.

Complaining may have been a fixed habit with the doctor, but he had certainly overworked it during the first weeks of his stay at the Lazy R. If he found any enjoyment in riding, he gave no evidence of it. The days were always too hot, or too windy. He could always find some objection to the horse he rode. The entire West, in his opinion, was crude and unattractive. He ridiculed the western style of dress, along with Jim's cowboy songs.

Like many others before him, the doctor had made many attempts to involve Jim in a discussion of technical subjects. He had met with little success along that line, however. Through long experience, Jim had developed rare skill in avoiding dangerous topics of conversation. Many a visitor at the Lazy

R had discovered that Jim Dawson was not as dense as he sometimes appeared.

One day Jim had taken the party of riders far up Rattlesnake Gulch. The doctor had been complaining bitterly about the heat, when he suddenly grew silent. A thought had flashed into his mind. And he was so pleased with it that he almost smiled. He would certainly take some of the conceit out of this smug cowpoke before this day was over.

The riders had been cooling oft in the shade of a big poplar tree before the return trip. Conversation had been in keeping with the laziness of the day, and the doctor had been strangely silent. He was only waiting, however, for a favorable opportunity.

"Dawson," he finally asked when he could wait no longer, "what is your opinion of relativity?"

"Relativity?" Jim repeated, thoughtfully flicking the ash from his cigarette. "Hmmm. Now I reckon you're referrin' to that feller what says things ain't what they seem to be, or somethin' like that. An' if my memory ain't gone back on me, his first name's Einstein. Nope, I ain't got no opinion regardin' him. You see, doctor, I figure as how it don't make good sense to be formin' opinions 'bout a feller I ain't never seen." A look of disgust clouded the doctor's face, as he mopped away the perspiration.

"What a beastly day," he muttered.

"Yep," Jim cheerfully agreed, "it is right warm. But it ain't nothin' to what it can be sometimes. I'll never forget the day I was up in Thunder Canyon looking for some stray yearlin's. You see, that was a long time ago, 'fore I got hooked up with the Lazy R. It was so blasted hot I could've cooked an egg on the seat o' my saddle.

"I was lookin' for a shady place to rest my hoss when I seen an Injun comin' down the canyon. I was rollin' a cigarette when he comes up to me an' smiles like we was old friends. I says somethin' 'bout it bein' a mighty hot day. He looks at me sort o' queer like, an' says, 'Heap fine day.' Reckon I must've looked right queer myself 'bout that time. I knowed Injuns liked a joke, but he didn't look much like he was jokin'. An', with me sweatin' like a race horse, that Injun looked as cool as a toad in a hailstorm. Well, we talks awhile, then I rides on up the canyon. But I can't get that Injun out o' my mind. An' the more I thinks 'bout him, the less I seem to mind the heat. The sun ain't changed none, but I don't seem to mind it so much.

"Now it's a funny thing' bout them Injuns," Jim went on.

"It don't seem to make no difference to 'em how hot it is, or how cold it is. You never hear 'em grumblin' 'bout it. They're mighty interestin' folks, when you git to know 'em.',

"Thanks," snapped the doctor, "I'm not interested in knowing the filthy heathen." Jim ignored the doctor's sharp return.

"Just the same," he said, "a feller can learn a lot from 'em. I'll admit they ain't as clean as they might be. But I don't' reckon we'd be much cleaner, if we had to live where they do. You know, water ain't none too plenty in this country. Anyways, they're smart folks, them Injuns is. They're too smart to be fussin' 'bout things they ain't got no power to change.

"Now them Injuns ain't got nothin', accordin' to our way o' lookin' at it. Most of 'em ain't got nothin' more'n what they can carry on their backs. They ain't got none o' the things white folks think they have to have to make 'em happy. Half the time they ain't even got 'nuff to eat, but you don't hear 'em complainin' 'bout it. Take old Foxear now; I've knowed that Injun for more'n thirty years, an, I ain't never heard a word o' complaint out o' him 'bout anything." The doctor's gaze seemed fixed upon something in the far distance. He was silent.

Jim Dawson stretched himself, and said, "Well, folks, I reckon we'd better be hittin' the trail for home."

The doctor was scheduled to leave the ranch the following day. But he stayed on; and, to everyone's amazement, he appeared to enjoy himself during the next two weeks. One of the guests was watching Jim Dawson saddle the horses one morning.

"Jim," he said, "that was quite interesting, what you told us about the Indians the other day. And it seems to have had a very good effect upon the doctor." Jim smiled.

"Well," he drawled, "the doc's not a bad sort. There's him. You see, it takes 'em a long time to find out the Lord didn't send 'em here to make the world over accordin' to their own notions."

One Way Out

Jim Dawson had taken the guests of the Lazy R up to the mesa this afternoon. Supper had been a delight, in the mellow glow of a gorgeous sunset. But bewildering as that colorful spectacle had been, it had not interfered with full justice being done to Jim's culinary skill. Now they were watching the magic change of day into night. They would return to the ranch by moonlight.

When the golden orb finally rose slowly over the distant mountain ridge, a hush fell upon the little group about the smoldering fire. It was a new experience for most of those present, and they were filled with speechless wonder. This was especially true of the three young schoolteachers from Indiana who were on their first visit to this vast and mystic land.

It was one of these who finally broke the silence. "What a night romance!" she said, in a wistful voice.

"Perfect, I would call it," came from one of her companions.

"Speaking of romance," one of the older guests said, "I'll bet our genial guide has had many interesting experiences along that line. It must be quite a problem to cope success-fully with the impressionable females who so often invade the dude ranches." Jim Dawson rolled a cigarette in silence.

"How about it, Jim?" inquired another. "I've heard some queer tales myself about the lovelorn amazons who prey upon the unsuspecting cowboy. Surely you must have encountered some of them."

"Nope," was Jim's hesitant response, "nothin' to speak of."

"Now, Jim, you're holding out on us. That isn't fair."

"Well," Jim finally drawled, "there was one gal that shore had me on the run for a while. She come nigh runnin' me off the ranch. It come out all right though, when she seen she'd been playin' with dynamite. There wasn't nobody hurt." Jim shifted his position, giving the impression that he had no desire to pursue such a delicate subject.

"Couldn't you tell us how it worked out?" the guest persisted. Jim thoughtfully scratched his ear before replying.

"Oh, I don't reckon it could hurt none to tell 'bout it," he drawled. "Now, you see, this was a long time ago, 'fore I had much dealin' with womenfolks. It was my first summer here, so you might say I wasn't broke yet. Anyways, when this gal from Chicago breezed in here, she sort o' perched herself on me, if you git what I mean.

"She was down at the corral the first thing in the mornin', an' all day long I couldn't hardly turn 'round without steppin' on her. She couldn't even trust me to git to my cabin after dark. Nope, she had to come taggin' 'long. She'd sit on the steps an' keep me singin' till it wasn't hardly worthwhile goin' to bed. An' she hadn't been here more'n a couple o' days till she begins callin' me sugary names. Now I ain't never had no objections to sweets, but I wasn't hankerin' after no sich offerin's from another man's wife. But it was honey this, an' sweetheart that, till I felt sticky all over."

"Was she living with her husband?" someone asked, when Jim stopped to roll a cigarette.

"Yep," he drawled. "Leastwise, she was supposed to be. Wasn't workin' too hard at it though, accordin' to the things she told. Had plenty o' money, an' most everything a woman might want, but she wasn't no ways satisfied. Claimed her man didn't understand her, didn't give her what she was sufferin' for."

"What was that?" someone asked, when Jim paused to light his cigarette from the slowly dying fire.

"Romance," he replied. Then, as the blue smoke curled lazily over the brim of his well-weathered Stetson, he continued.

"Well, she'd booked for only two weeks, so I stuck it out somehow. But when I seen she had no notion o' leavin' when them two weeks was gone, I give up' Then I puts it up to the Boss pronto. I tells him he'd have to git somebody else on my job, 'cause I was quittin'. 'What's wrong?' he says to me. 'I thought you liked the job.'

"'I did,' I tells him, till that gal from Chicago blows in.' Then I tells him how it was. 'Just last night,' I says, 'she follers me over to the cabin. She sits there on the steps cryin', 'cause she says she's unhappy. 'Course that's too bad, Boss, but it ain't my funeral. An' seein' as how I can't shake her off my trail without insultin' her, there ain't nothin' left for me to do but move out.'

"'Now listen, Jim,' the Boss says, 'you can't leave me in a hole this way. You know there ain't nobody to take your place. An' we'll be closin' in a couple more weeks. It ain't goin' to hurt you none to be nice to the gal a little longer. Ain't you smart 'nuff to handle such things without insultin' folks?'

"Well, I knowed I couldn't find a better job, 'cause my cowpunchin' days was gone. An' the Boss had been mighty good to me, so I cools off an' agrees to stick. That night, after I'd given the folks a few songs, I lays the old geetar on the steps an' goes in the house. Then slips out the kitchen door an' goes over to the cook's cabin. We sit there chewin' the rag till the lights was all out in the big house. I then ambles over to my own cabin, feelin' right pleased with myself. I was goin' to git a good night's sleep for a change."

"And your troubles were over," one of the guests remarked, when Jim began to roll another cigarette. "I suppose the poor soul took her sorrowful departure the following day."

"Yep," Jim returned, with a grin. "Yep, she left the next day all right, but my troubles wasn't over yet. When I got to the cabin, what do you think I found there?" He paused for a moment, while his silent audience waited. "Well, there was that gal sittin' on the steps with the old geetar in her lap. She looks up at me an' smiles, sort o' sad like. She had mighty pretty eyes an' she shore knowed how to use 'em.

"'You forgot this,' she says, handin' me the old relic. 'Just as you'll be forgettin' me when I'm gone, I suppose.' Well, I just stands there lookin' at her, not knowin' what to say. You see she wasn't hard to look at. Then she says, 'Sit down here beside me.' I had to sit right close, 'cause there wasn't too much room on them steps.

"Then she takes hold o' my hand, an' says to me, 'Jim, darlin', I think you're wonderful, but I know you don't feel that way 'bout me.' She's lookin' up at the moon, while I sits there not sayin' a word, just wishin' I was some place I wasn't.

"After a while she looks at me, an' says, 'I wonder why you never married?' 'Ain't never said I had'nt been married,' I says, havin' a tough time keepin' my face straight. 'Oh,' she says, 'I didn't know.'

"'Didn't reckon you would,' I says. 'Ain't many folks what knows 'bout it. You see, I had sort o' tough luck with my wives an' I don't like talkin' 'bout it.'

"'Wives!' she sort o' gasps, droppin' my hand like it was a rattlesnake. 'Yep,' I says, 'six of 'em. Three went out sort o' natural like, but the last three lost their minds. Crazy as loons, they was.' Well, that gal lets out one wild yell an' makes for the house like a scared rabbit. An' that was the last I seen of her."

The Tale of the Rat

"Mr. Dawson, will you please tell me what a pack rat is?" That question had come from a new arrival at the Lazy R'

"Ain't you never seen a pack rat?" was Jim's cautious return.

"No, I never have. But I've heard they were very destructive."

"Well, I wouldn't say they was specially destructive," Jim drawled. "Anyways, not the ones we have 'round here"

"Oh!" the guest exclaimed, in evident horror, "where do they stay?"

"Now, miss, that's somethin' nobody can't never be sure 'bout. You see, a pack rat don't never stay long in one place. He likes to move 'round, sort o' like the Injuns."

"But how do they differ from ordinary rats?" the guest persisted. "What do they look like?"

"Well," Jim replied, carefully rolling a cigarette, "he looks a lot like most any other kind o' tat, 'cept he's bigger an' powerful strong. You might say he was a special brand an' a mighty smart critter too. He don't hang 'round houses an' barns much. Reckon that's 'cause he don't trust us folks. Bein' the pirate o' the rat tribe, he don't mix with the common rats."

"A pirate! Just how do you mean?" someone asked, when Jim picked up the guitar again.

"Well, you see, he's a natural-born robber," Jim returned.' "He'll steal most anything he can pack off. It's a mighty good thing to keep your doors shut nights. You can't never tell what one o' them critters might take a notion to walk off with. I lost a good pair o' boots that way onct."

"What in the world would a rat want with boots?" someone asked.

"Well, I reckon he figured as how a boot could make mighty snug sleepin' quarters."

"But why would he want two of them?"

"One for himself an' one for the wife, most likely. Reckon that pair didn't believe in sleepin' together."

"Did you ever find the boots?" was the next question, when the laughter had subsided.

"Nope, never seen 'em again," Jim replied. "More'n likely that outfit was livin' back in the hills 'mongst the rocks. An' them rocks gits mighty cold in winter. Them pirates was aimin' to be comfortable. I was hoppin' mad 'bout losin' them boots. But," he added, thoughtfully gazing skyward, "pack rats is sort o' like human bein's, in a way. There's good ones 'mongst' em."

"Now what good could anyone find in a rat?" someone demanded.

"Well," Jim drawled, "we had one round here onct that right decent feller. 'Course, he wasn't 'bove packin' off anything he wanted, but he always give something in exchange. It wasn't always a fair deal, but sometimes it was a mighty good one.

"There wasn't no screens on my cabin that summer, so Mr. Packer had the run o' the place. But this feller never took nothin' without comin' back the next night with somethin' in trade. It was right funny, the things he'd pick up 'round here, most of 'em bein' things the womenfolks had lost. Yep, everything from hairpins to earrings. Now I reckon you won't believe it, but that feller traded me a ruby earring for one o' my socks."

"It sounds interesting, Jim," someone remarked. "Tell us about it."

"Well, as I was sayin' " Jim continued, "this feller wasn't no robber. He was a trader. Sometimes I wasn't to pleased 'bout the things he took, but it was sort o' interestin' to see what he'd be packin' in the next night. Well, I was readin' a story the night after he'd stole the sock. It was so interestin' I plumb lost track of time.

"When I stops in the middle o' the story to roll a cigarette, I seen somethin' in the doorway. An', shore 'nuff, it was Mr. Pack Rat, an' he had somethin' in his mouth. I just naturally looked for him to make tracks when he seen me sittin' there starin' at him, but he didn't.

"Nope, that feller looks at me sort o' friendly like an' trots over to the bed. He stops right where he'd found my socks an' there he drops that thing out o' his mouth. Then he rots out o' the door, switchin' his tail, much as to say, "Now we're square, old-timer."

"Well, I've lost interest in stories, so I gits up to see what the old boy had dug up as an offerin'. When I gits the dirt off the thing, I find it's a gold earring, with a red stone in it. Nobody ever claimed it. So I sold it for 'nuff to keep me in socks the rest o' my days."

"Now, Jim, that was quite an interesting tale," said one of the guests, "but you don't expect us to believe it, do you?"

"I ain't got but one answer to that," Jim returned, with a grin. "Jim Dawson won't be losin' no sleep, no matter which way you take it."

A Complex Problem

Even Jim Dawson's guitar seemed to sound more melancholy than usual tonight. One more day and the guest season at the Lazy R would be closed.

"Well, Jim," someone remarked, as the conversation lagged, "I suppose you will be happy this time tomorrow."

"Why so?" Jim inquired, carefully rolling a cigarette.

"Because," the dude returned, "there'll be no dumb dudes to annoy you for months to come."

"Wrong on the first count," Jim replied. "I ain't neverbeen annoyed by the folks what comes here."

"Well," someone remarked, "I should think your vacation would be far more enjoyable. You must find some of the guests very troublesome at times."

"Nope," Jim replied, "I ain't never thought o' 'em as troublesome. There was one that was what a feller might've called somethin' of a problem. But it wasn't her fault. It was mostly on account o' her architecture."

"Please tell us about it," came in a chorus from the dudes.

"Well," Jim began, "this gal was from New York, if my memory ain't gone back on me. She'd got a notion in her red head that she wasn't goin' to like me. But 'fore she left, we was as chummy as a couple o' chipmunks on a rainy day. She was most nigh as long as a yard o' pump water an, not much heftier. She stood a good half-foot above me, an, I ain't never been accused o' bein' so short on altitude neither. I was in the corral when she comes lopin' up to me an' says, 'you're Jim Dawson, I presume?'

"'Pre-which?' I says, lookin, down to see what she's standin' on. Then she takes a good. look at me 'fore she says, 'You're Jim Dawson all right.' 'Now I,m right glad you guessed it, miss,' I says to her. 'Yes,' she says, 'I've heard about you. You're one o' them fellers what thinks they're funny, an' I'm warnin' you not to try any o' your funny stuff on me. Now what horse do I git?'

"'Ever straddle a hoss before?' I asks her, just as though I ain't heard her flatterin' remarks. 'No,' she snaps, 'but I want a good one.' 'Well, miss,' I says, 'we ain't got no other brand on the Lazy R. The only trouble is, there ain't many of 'em what knows how to break a person to ride.' She looks at me sort o' queer like as I walks off. 'So,' I says to myself, 'the gal's heard 'bout me an' she's made up her mind she ain't goin' to like me. Now ain't that just too bad.'

"Now I picks Flossy for the gal, 'cause Flossy was safe 'nuff for a baby to ride, an' a good-sized hoss too. Well, when I got the saddle on that gal throws a leg over Flossy like she was steppin' over a chair. I come mighty nigh smilin', but I didn't.

"'This one won't do,' the gal says. 'I want one that fits me.' I lets the stirrups down to the last notch, but they was still too short. 'Well, miss,' I says, 'that's a natural 'nuff desire all right. But it just don't seem like Nature designed hosses with the required specifications in mind.'

"Well, folks," Jim concluded, "that gal must've looked at me a couple o' minutes' fore she said anythin'. Then she smiles, sort o' uncertain like, an' says to me, 'Jim Dawson, I believe I'm goin' to like you after all.' Well, I just smiles back at her, an' says, 'Now don't let that bother you, miss. Quite a lot o' folks has been in the same boat an' none of 'em ever sunk.' "

The Last Roundup

Jim Dawson had given many hints of his long-planned retirement, but no one had taken him seriously. Certainly no one at the Lazy R was prepared for the manner of his going. One morning after the guest season had closed, the Boss found a bit of paper pinned outside his door. On it was the following, scribbled with a pencil:

Deer boss.

They say theres a end to everything. Reckon this is it tween me an the Lazy R. I ain't never been much of a hand at sayin gudby–so well be gone fore your up. We are on our way to the last roundup, barney an me. Take gud care o the hosses an keep the duds off old Sentnal. Solong now.

JIM

www.ingramcontent.com/pod-product-compliance
Lightning Source LLC
Chambersburg PA
CBHW032023090426
42741CB00006B/715